The Diaconate in Ecumenical Perspective

Ecclesiology, Liturgy and Practice

EDITED BY

— D. MICHAEL JACKSON —

Sacristy
Press

Sacristy Press
PO Box 612, Durham, DH1 9HT

www.sacristy.co.uk

First published in 2019 by Sacristy Press, Durham

Sacristy Limited, registered in England & Wales, number 7565667

British Library Cataloguing-in-Publication Data
A catalogue record for the book is available from the British Library

Paperback ISBN 978-1-78959-035-7
Hardback ISBN 978-1-78959-055-5

Foreword

The diaconate has evolved over the centuries and continues to adapt to current needs and situations. As part of the fulfilment of a baptismal identity and vocation that many have discerned, God's call to people to serve as a deacon is not static. It is dynamic and an ongoing dialogue between God and the Church that simultaneously enhances the Church and the individual.

The international Anglican–Roman Catholic–Ukrainian Catholic conference on the diaconate, held in Regina, Saskatchewan, Canada, in May 2018 took as its departure point the recognition that all of our churches have a threefold ministry including the diaconate, and that diaconal ministry is being explored by all of us in significant ways at the present time. It was and is our conviction that we can learn from scholars of our own and of our dialogue partners' traditions as we engage in serious reflection about the diaconate and identify new ways of collaborating in diaconal ministry.

In 2016, Archbishop Justin of Canterbury and Pope Francis met in Rome with the members of the International Anglican–Roman Catholic Commission for Unity and Mission and asked, among other things: "Will you strive to be united in preaching the gospel in word and deed and united in serving those who are most vulnerable and marginalized?" We believe that the diaconate is an integral part of the Church's mission to those on the peripheries.

This book of essays published by Sacristy Press is based on presentations from our three traditions given at the 2018 conference. In addition, we welcome the inclusion of chapters on the Lutheran and Methodist diaconates: these underscore the significance of the title, *The Diaconate in Ecumenical Perspective*. We pray that this book will help raise the profile of deacons in our church and provide a vocational stimulus and greater vision for the diaconate in the world today.

✠Donald Bolen

Archbishop of Regina

+ Robert Hardwick

Bishop of Qu'Appelle

+ Bryan Bayda, CSsR

Eparch of Saskatoon

Preface

In 2011, the Anglican Diocese of Qu'Appelle and the Roman Catholic Archdiocese of Regina—covering the southernmost part of the Canadian province of Saskatchewan—entered into a covenant relationship, where they committed to working together "in jointly building up the body of Christ" through shared activities, study, prayer and parish exchanges. The covenant provided for expanding the relationship to the other dioceses of both churches in the civil province and to the Ukrainian Catholic and Lutheran churches as well, a process under way in 2019.

One shared interest of the originating dioceses has been the order of deacons, with diaconal programmes in place for over three decades in the case of the Diocese of Qu'Appelle, more recently for the Archdiocese of Regina. Collaboration in diaconal study and formation led to the initiative by the two dioceses, joined by the Ukrainian Catholic Eparchy of Saskatoon, of convening an international, inter-church conference on the diaconate. This took place in May 2018 at Campion College, the Jesuit-affiliated college at the University of Regina.

The conference attracted a hundred people from the three churches, including four bishops, eight priests, fifty-five deacons, and a number of diaconal candidates and lay people, from seven Canadian provinces, six US states, England, Scotland and New Zealand. Bishop Robert Hardwick of Qu'Appelle and Archbishop Donald Bolen of Regina co-chaired the conference, with Bishop Bryan Bayda of the Ukrainian Catholic Eparchy of Saskatoon as a session chair. Archbishop Bolen observed that

> this international conference was a new venture in our covenantal relationship, building on the fact that both our Churches have a threefold ministry including the diaconate, and that diaconal ministry is being explored in significant ways by both Churches, including our respective dioceses, at the present time.

Entitled "The Ministry of the Deacon: Word and Sacrament, Charity and Justice", the conference featured leading authorities on the diaconate from Canada, the United States and the United Kingdom. They addressed nine topics:

- The Theological Basis of the Diaconate
- The Conundrum of the Transitional Diaconate
- Women and the Diaconate
- The Diaconate as Ecumenical Opportunity
- The Diaconate in the Orthodox and Eastern Catholic Churches
- The Prophetic Ministry of the Deacon
- The Deacon in the Worshipping Community
- Diaconal Formation
- Diaconal Relationships

Most of the essays in the present volume are based on presentations given at the 2018 Regina conference. However, we welcome two much-appreciated additional contributions on the Methodist and Lutheran diaconal orders, reflecting the widespread interest in the ministry of the deacon in Christian churches around the world—truly ecumenical in scope.

The organizers of the conference and the contributors to this book thank the Faith, Worship and Ministry Department of the Anglican Church of Canada and the Archdiocese of Regina for generous grants which made them both possible. We also express our gratitude to Sacristy Press, particularly Richard Hilton, Operations Director, and Natalie Watson, Commissioning Editor, for their support and guidance as *The Diaconate in Ecumenical Perspective* took form. We trust that this book will further the understanding and appreciation of the ministry of the deacon in our churches.

(Deacon Canon) D. Michael Jackson
Conference Coordinator and General Editor
Regina, Canada, June 2019

Contributors

Frederick C. (Fritz) Bauerschmidt is a deacon of the Roman Catholic Archdiocese of Baltimore (ordained 2007) and Professor of Theology at Loyola University, Maryland. He is the author of several books, including *Thomas Aquinas: Faith, Reason, and Following Christ* (Oxford University Press), *Catholic Theology: An Introduction* (with James Buckley, Wiley Publishers), and *The Deacon's Ministry of Liturgy* (Liturgical Press).

Josephine (Phina) Borgeson was ordained deacon in 1974 and serves in the Episcopal Diocese of Northern California. Her community work centres on food system ministries and related environmental concerns, including interfaith networking and consulting. She is involved in ministry development and education, mentoring new deacons and teaching those preparing to be deacons. She is a past president of the North American Association for the Diaconate.

Rosalind Brown, after a few years living in the United States, during which she was ordained, trained people for ordination in the United Kingdom. She was a Residentiary Canon at Durham Cathedral from 2005 to 2018, where she had oversight of the nave, or public, ministry of the cathedral. Prior to that, she chaired the Diocese of Salisbury's working party on the ministry of deacons, edited the Salisbury report on the Distinctive Diaconate, and is author of several books on ministry and preaching, including *Being a Deacon Today* (Canterbury Press, 2005).

Brian A. Butcher, a sub-deacon in the Ukrainian Greco-Catholic Church, is Lecturer and Research Fellow in Eastern Christian Studies in the Faculty of Theology at the University of St Michael's College (Toronto School of Theology). He is part of the Metropolitan Andrey Sheptysky Institute of Eastern Christian Studies. His second book is *Liturgical Theology after*

Schmemann: An Orthodox Reading of Paul Ricoeur (Fordham University Press, 2018).

David Clark became a member of the British Methodist Diaconal Order in 2005. Prior to that, he worked as a Methodist minister in Sheffield and London and as a senior lecturer in community education at Westhill College, Birmingham. He played a leading role in the emergence of the Christian Community Movement, set up the Christians in Public Life Programme, and founded the Human City Institute. His latest book is *The Gift of a Renewed Diaconate—and the Contribution of British Methodism* (FastPrint Publishing, 2018).

Susanne Watson Epting was ordained deacon in the Episcopal Church of the USA in 1989. She served as a board member of the Association for Episcopal Deacons for eight years and as its director for ten. Active over many years in ministry development, she became an assistant to the bishop, working with individuals and congregations. Her book *Unexpected Consequences—The Diaconate Renewed* was published by Morehouse Publishing in 2015.

D. Michael Jackson, ordained in 1977, is the longest-serving deacon in the Anglican Church of Canada. He is author of *The Diaconate Renewed: Service, Word and Worship* and *The Deacon in the Worshipping Community* (Diocese of Qu'Appelle website), coordinates a network of Anglican and Roman Catholic deacons, and is a reviewer of diaconal publications. He serves as deacon at St Paul's Cathedral in Regina and is a canon of the Diocese of Qu'Appelle.

Gloria Marie Jones, OP, served eleven years as Congregational Prioress for the Dominican Sisters of Mission San Jose, an international Roman Catholic community with sisters in Mexico and the United States. She received her MA in Religious Studies from the Catholic University of America and served the Catholic Community at Stanford University as Director of Faith Formation and Chaplain. As the daughter of a deacon, she brings keen interest to the question of diaconal ministry in the Church today.

Anne Keffer was consecrated a Lutheran deaconess in 1964. As Director of Christian Education and Youth Ministry, she served large urban congregations in Ontario and a rural team ministry in Nova Scotia. Receiving her MEd in Counselling, she was a university chaplain in Saskatchewan and Ontario. While she was the Executive Director of the Prairie Centre for Ecumenism in Saskatoon, she was called by the Deaconess Community, ELCA, to be its directing deaconess in Chicago, where she served for seven years.

Maylanne Maybee has been a deacon in the Anglican Church of Canada since 1978. She is an educator, social justice activist, ecumenist, and writer on the diaconate and ecclesiology. She was Principal of the Centre for Christian Studies, a theological school in Winnipeg for diaconal candidates, and is now Interim Principal at the United Theological College in Montreal. She edited and contributed to *All Who Minister: New Ways of Serving God's People* (ABC Publishing, 2001).

George E. Newman, ordained to the Roman Catholic diaconate in 1987, served as Director of Diaconate Formation in Toronto from 1992 to 2002. He established a diaconate formation programme in the Diocese of St Catharines in 2003, retiring from this position in 2017. Deacon Newman currently assists Newman Theological College in Edmonton as instructor in diaconate programmes. He has assisted with the establishment of diaconate programmes in a number of dioceses.

Alison Peden was a medievalist at St Hilda's College, Oxford, before moving to Scotland in 1990, where she taught at the Universities of Glasgow and Stirling. She trained in the Scottish Episcopal Church and at Edinburgh University for her ordination in 2002. When serving as Rector of Holy Trinity, Stirling, she became involved in the formation of ordinands. She was appointed Provincial Director of Ordinands in 2011, with oversight of recruitment and selection for ministry throughout the Scottish Episcopal Church.

E. Louise Williams is a deacon in the Evangelical Lutheran Church in America and was consecrated a deaconess in 1967. After serving in parish ministry, she served on the staff of the Lutheran Deaconess Association (LDA), retiring as Executive Director in 2008. She is past president of Diakonia World Federation and Diakonia of the Americas and Caribbean. She teaches Theology of Diaconal Ministry at Valparaiso University in Indiana.

Contents

INTRODUCTION

The Diaconate in Ecumenical Perspective

D. Michael Jackson

Diakonia, diaconate, deacon, deaconess. These words resonate in the lexicon of the Christian churches. In some historical periods, there has been agreement on their meaning. *Diakonia* was understood as a Greek term for service, humble or even menial service. The *diaconate* was the third order of ordained ministers in a hierarchical church—the lowest of three rungs on an ecclesiastical career ladder. For most of the second millennium, *deacons* were apprentice priests and liturgical functionaries. *Deaconesses?* While their ancient origins as female ministers may be obscure, they re-emerged in the nineteenth century as the equivalent of religious social workers. The revival of the (male) "permanent" diaconate in the late twentieth century after the Second Vatican Council took some of its cues from the deaconess movement, leading to a perception of the deacon as a minister of outreach and social justice.

However, these interpretations of deacon-related terminology have been questioned and in many cases revised, as scholarship on the diaconate has developed in tandem with the revival and renewal of the order of deacons in churches around the world. Take, for example, the understanding of *diakonia.* Since the 1990s, the Australian Roman Catholic scholar John N. Collins has challenged the long-accepted interpretation that this Greek New Testament word denoted humble service. *Diakonia*, argues Collins, meant much more than that— commissioned minister, ambassador, intermediary, mediator, agent of the bishop.[1] Several contributors to this volume draw attention to the implications of Collins' work. Indeed, Maylanne Maybee prefers to "stay with the Greek word *diakonia*", as, she says, we have not "settled yet on a definitive English translation" of this term so rich in its connotations.

Theology of the diaconate

Without the theological backbone of *diakonia*, we will be at a loss to understand the identity and purpose of the ministerial order of deacons. Rosalind Brown tackles it head-on. Acknowledging how unsure we have been about "just what or who a deacon is", she takes a Trinitarian and Christological approach to diaconal ordination. She welcomes the influence of John Collins's research on the evolution of the Church of England's ordinal from the "inferior office" of 1662 to the "heralds of Christ's kingdom" in 2000. "An explicit Spirit-based pneumatological underpinning," she says, "gives added impetus to the deacon's role in the Church's mission of proclaiming the Kingdom of God."

Frederick C. Bauerschmidt complements Canon Brown's Anglican view with a lucid analysis of the Roman Catholic theology of diaconal ordination. He contrasts the approach of the Vatican II decree *Ad gentes*, which saw the ordination of a deacon as recognizing supposed "diaconal" qualities already present in the candidate, with that council's *Lumen gentium*, where the sacrament "brings about a new state of being" in the ordinands, effectively launching them into diaconal ministry. *Ad gentes* presumed that we clearly knew what diaconal ministry was. But this is no longer the case. Indicating his preference for the *Lumen gentium* model, Deacon Bauerschmidt says that "this freeing of *diakonia* from a monolithic model of menial service" leads to flexibility in discerning vocations and encourages variety in forms of diaconal ministry.

The "transitional" diaconate

The renewed appreciation of the theology of the diaconate inevitably calls into question the continued existence of the "transitional" diaconate in the Anglican, Roman Catholic and Eastern traditions—the passage through the order of deacons for a year, more or less, of those to be ordained presbyter or priest. Although the earliest practice of the Church had been "direct" ordination to the diaconate, the priesthood and the episcopate, by the fifth century "sequential" ordination into successive orders was replacing it. To be a priest or presbyter, one first had to be a deacon. To be a bishop, one had to be a priest. The doctrine of "cumulative" ordination took this a stage further: not only was one order a preparation for the next, but each order incorporated the previous one. Rosalind Brown calls it "the 'Russian dolls' model of ordination . . . inside some baptized Christians there is a deacon, inside some deacons there is a priest, and inside some priests there is a bishop."

Others take issue with the theory and practice of sequential and cumulative ordination. Susanne Watson Epting notes how the ordination rite in the 1979 American Episcopal *Book of Common Prayer* (like the Church of England's 2000 ordinal) removed the hierarchical, "inferior order", connotation of the diaconate and restored it as a distinctive vocation. The 1979 Prayer Book emphasized the centrality of baptism as the foundation of all ministry—a point also raised by Maylanne Maybee in her essay on the ecumenical scope of the diaconate. Both authors acknowledge that many priests cling to the notion that they are deacons too, but, says Deacon Maybee, this is "through baptism, not through an earlier act of ordination". Alison Peden asserts that, while all ministry is based on baptism, the vocation, training, formation and roles of the deacon are different from those for the priest: candidates should be directly ordained to either order. Looking at the formation of Roman Catholic transitional deacons, George Newman comments, "one would be led to wonder, if he is not going to engage in traditional deacon ministry, why ordain him a deacon".

Women and the diaconate

The "he" and "him" mentioned by Deacon Newman raise the intriguing question of why not "she" and "her". Ecumenical scholarship, after much debate, generally accepts that in the third through the seventh centuries— and in some cases well beyond—women *were* ordained to the diaconate. They were usually called "deaconesses" and found mostly in the East. The issue, explains Ukrainian Catholic scholar Brian A. Butcher, is not the historical existence of female deacons, but its theological implications, then and now. He cautions that "the Christian East has served as a quarry from which scholars have mined evidence for a predominantly Western debate", whereas opinion and practice have varied widely among the Oriental and Orthodox churches, and the partial revival of the female diaconate there is not without controversy.

That said, it appears that female deacons in the early Church functioned in parallel with their male counterparts, albeit ministering primarily to women. The decline of the diaconate in general prompted an accelerated decline of the female diaconate, until it nearly disappeared altogether, even in the East. After all, if the diaconate was merely a transitional office on the way to the priesthood, from which women were barred, why should, indeed how *could*, women be deacons? Of course, women's *ministry* did not disappear—far from it. Religious orders for women as well as men spread throughout the Church during the Middle Ages. As Anne Keffer and E. Louise Williams describe in their chapter, the present-day diaconates in the Lutheran churches originated in the deaconess movement in nineteenth-century Germany, dealing with the social problems stemming from the Industrial Revolution. Maylanne Maybee notes how the movement spread to the Church of England and then to other churches of the Anglican Communion.

Some provinces of the Anglican Communion began ordaining women to the diaconate in the 1970s, and female deacons have now largely replaced deaconesses. Lutheran deaconesses, like their Anglican counterparts, were not ordained—terms such as "commissioned" or "consecrated" were used. It is to the Roman Catholic Church that attention is now turning. Gloria Marie Jones, daughter of a deacon, poignantly notes that, while "deacons are called to animate and sacramentalize the Church's call to service", only half of her Church, those who are male, are currently able to fulfil this role. Sister Gloria was present at the Vatican in 2016, when Pope Francis announced his intention to set up a commission to study the question of women deacons. The commission submitted its report at the beginning of 2019. As Dr Butcher observes, the Eastern-Rite Catholic churches will "wait to see what transpires in the Latin Church".

Ecumenical views of the diaconate

Whether female or male, the diaconate is a current topic in inter-church dialogue. Part 4 of this volume appropriately begins with Brian Butcher's "theological considerations of the diaconate in the Orthodox and Eastern Catholic Churches". If the Eastern-Rite churches are being "mined" for the history of women deacons, they also deserve to be for the diaconate in general. Even though their priests historically and today must first be ordained transitional deacons, the permanent diaconate continued in the Eastern churches despite its near extinction in the West. Compared to its Western counterpart, the diaconate in the East has been and remains extraordinarily complex. The four "ecclesial communions"—Assyrian, Oriental Orthodox, Eastern Orthodox and Eastern-Rite Catholic— demonstrate considerable differences in their respective approaches to the order of deacons. Even within these communions there are varied practices among the churches. The Western observer will note, however, the crucial importance of the deacon's liturgical role in all the branches of the Eastern tradition. This contrasts with the ambivalence in the West towards the deacon's place in worship. Indeed, the nature of the entire ministry of the deacon is the subject of debate within and among the churches.

In this context, it is helpful to look beyond those churches which have an episcopally-ordained diaconate within the historical threefold ministry—the Anglican, Roman Catholic and Eastern communions—to those with different patterns. David Clark is a member of the British Methodist Diaconal Order, which had its origins in a deaconess movement begun at the end of the nineteenth century, influenced by the Lutheran example. Interestingly, he was formerly a Methodist presbyter— effectively reversing the path of the transitional deacon in the episcopal churches! In his writings, Deacon Clark promotes the ecclesiology of a diaconal, servant church, where a renewed diaconate offers leadership to the laity in building a "kingdom community" to effect change in the world.

The chapter by Anne Keffer and Louise Williams is aptly named "Diaconates—the Lutheran Experience"; for in these "diaconates" (plural), there are echoes of the variety found in the Eastern churches. As we have already noted, the Lutheran diaconate stems from the influential deaconess movement in nineteenth-century Germany, which soon spread to the Scandinavian Lutheran churches and around the world. The Lutheran concept of *diakonia* is based on "unconditional service to the neighbour in need", which "leads inevitably to social change that restores, reforms and transforms"—a parallel with the "kingdom community" objective of the Methodist diaconate described by David Clark. Practices differ considerably between the national Lutheran churches: in some of them, deacons are ordained as part of a threefold ministry; in others, they are commissioned; in some, deacons have parish and liturgical functions; in others they are primarily involved in social service. The diaconate is in a state of flux in Lutheranism, notably in North America, stimulated by the ecumenical dialogue which is the *raison d'être* of this book.

Maylanne Maybee is a prime exponent of this dialogue, steeped as she is in the Anglican, Eastern, Lutheran and Reformed traditions. Her ecumenical view is a broad one, "*oikumene*, meaning the whole inhabited earth!" In ecclesial terms, she emphasizes the centrality of baptism for diaconal ordination, indeed all ordination. Her approach is that of "receptive ecumenism", where individual churches learn from the experience of the others. One of Deacon Maybee's most valuable insights is her synthesis of the traditional "servant" image and the reinterpretation of the deacon's ministry as agent, ambassador and herald. She sees a middle way between the polarized concepts of deacons as liturgical functionaries and as social activists—a classic Anglican compromise, albeit one based on the Anglican–Lutheran *Hanover Report*!

Prophetic ministry, worship and formation

Commenting on Ukrainian Catholic vespers celebrated at the conference which spawned this book, a leading deacon in the American Episcopal Church said:

> I found it numinous and beautiful. I could also understand that
> the role of deacons in these [Eastern rite] churches is primarily

liturgical. The call to "speak to the church about the needs, concerns and hopes of the world" is not a part of what they do.[2]

Eastern Christians would counter this by pointing out that "mercy, justice, and prophecy" are an integral part of *diakonia* and the diaconate in their tradition, while emphasizing the deacon's role in "worship, upbuilding the church, royal priesthood, and prayer and intercession".[3]

At the opposite pole, the deacon is seen primarily as an agent of social justice, bringing the gospel to bear on the manifest and manifold evils in society such as discrimination, oppression, racism, violence and poverty. The deacon reaches out to the marginalized, the homeless, the poor, and the disenfranchised, in short, the victims of social *injustice*. Particularly in North America, this interpretation of the diaconate often translates into quasi-political activism on issues such as economic disparity, the environment, and the status of indigenous peoples. At its limit, deacons may have no liturgical or preaching role at all, and their connection to the local Christian community such as a parish may be minimal, tenuous or even non-existent.

As we have seen, the Lutheran deaconess movement began as a response to the abysmal social conditions of the Industrial Revolution in nineteenth-century Germany. To this day, Anne Keffer and Louise Williams tell us, German Lutherans are reluctant to assign liturgical functions to deacons, perhaps rooted in Martin Luther's opposition to abuses in the Catholic Church, "where deacons had liturgical duties but ignored the needs of the poor." Certainly, the modern involvement of deacons in prison ministry, food banks, homeless shelters, and social service agencies has clear historical precedents.

However, as several of our contributors point out, a drawback to this concept of the deacon as the "purveyor of *diakonia*" is that it risks short-changing the vocation of *all* Christians, ordained and lay, to practise mercy, charity and justice. For Rosalind Brown, deacons are ordained to enable and resource "the ministry of all baptized Christians". Frederick Bauerschmidt questions Vatican II's *Ad gentes* model as implying "that the diaconate has a monopoly on *diakonia*". David Clark sees the primary calling of deacons as "enablers of the ministry of God's people to the world" rather than as one of "witness to service". Anne Keffer and Louise

Williams refer to the Lutheran view of "the deaconhood of all believers". Susanne Watson Epting reminds us that "we are all called to service at our baptism". Maylanne Maybee affirms that "the way I participate in the *diakonia* or sacred mission of Christ is through baptism". In other words, deacons are not the sole practitioners of *diakonia*—they are emblems and facilitators of the baptismal servant ministry of all.

Josephine Borgeson ponders how deacons may exercise leadership in the Church's prophetic activity. In the context of a creation marred by human consumerism, deacons can use the "shock value" of the parables of Jesus to challenge the postmodern view of reality—and the inevitable failures of the Church itself to live up to the gospel values it professes. Gloria Marie Jones pursues this theme in her reflections on "living the prophetic ministry of the deacon". She sees this as firmly grounded in spirituality, in the *communio* and *kenosis* of Jesus: the deacon is to be a bold prophetic voice to the whole Church and beyond to the world. The diaconate sacramentalizes Jesus' call to *diakonia* and the values of the kingdom of God: unity, inclusion and forgiveness.

Rosalind Brown sees a direct link with the liturgy: "diaconal ministry is a dynamic extension of eucharistic celebration". She focuses on the deacon's ministry of hospitality, with the provocative observation that welcoming people at the door of the church should be "the first role of the deacon in worship". The traditional diaconal roles of proclaiming the gospel, leading the prayers of the people and inviting them to share the Peace, preparing the Table and giving the Dismissal, derive from and follow up on that initial act of hospitality.

Frederick Bauerschmidt directs our attention to another function of the deacon: that of "liturgical *major domo*"—coordinating, facilitating and assisting all the ministers in the service. The challenge is to do so with flexibility and discretion, whilst maintaining a truly prayerful approach oneself. In my own chapter, I cite Roman Catholic texts, practices and writings as exemplars for the deacon's role in worship, which I argue is an essential component of diaconal ministry.

Three contributors discuss practices of formation for this ministry. Josephine Borgeson and Alison Peden underline the importance of the learning community and describe a formation programme based on skills and competencies. Canon Peden and George Newman show how the discernment and formation of the deacon differ substantially from those of the transitional deacon/priest.

—

There appears to be a growing ecumenical consensus on the diaconate. Views may differ on its origins: the venerable tradition that the first deacons were the "seven" referred to in Acts 6, including Philip and Stephen, is no longer accepted by most contemporary scholarship (even though it is cited in the ordinals of the Roman Catholic and Eastern churches)—evidence points to the emergence of the order of deacons later in the first century.[4] Similarly, there is debate over whether women were ordained deacons in the early Church, and if so, whether they should be again, and what form their ministry was then and should be now.[5]

On the other hand, there is a widely shared opinion that we should not, indeed cannot, replicate in our era what the diaconate, male or female, may have been in past millennia. The office of deacon has developed and evolved, especially since Vatican II. The relatively recent interpretation of the diaconate as service to others and social outreach is now clearly associated with diaconal ministry, even if this does not fully correspond to the original meaning of *diakonia*. In the same vein, churches reviving the female diaconate cannot expect it to be different from or subordinate to that of male deacons, as seems to have been the case in the early Church (even though Eastern churches may be reluctant to adapt to what they see as transient cultural norms). The deacon is called to a ministry in the *contemporary* Church.

That ministry is being liberated from stereotypes, ranging from an agent of humble service to a transitional liturgical functionary. The contributions to this book provide ample evidence of the rich variety, flexibility, depth and potential of the order of deacons in today's churches. Of course, within and between Christian traditions emphases will vary and diaconal roles will differ. Yet this classic Roman Catholic description is surely valid today and for all: "Deacons serve in a balanced and integrated threefold ministry of Word, Sacrament and Charity."[6]

Notes

[1] John N. Collins, *Diakonia: Re-interpreting the Ancient Sources* (New York, Oxford: Oxford University Press, 1990); *Deacons and the Church: Making Connections between Old and New* (Leominster: Gracewing; Harrisburg, PA: Morehouse, 2002); and *Diakonia Studies: Critical Issues in Ministry* (New York, Oxford: Oxford University Press, 2014).

[2] Deacon Pam Nesbit, in *Diakoneo*, quarterly magazine of the Association for Episcopal Deacons, August 2018.

[3] See my discussion in *The Diaconate Renewed: Service, Word and Worship*, Diocese of Qu'Appelle, revised March 2019, pp. 19–20 and 25–26. <https://quappelle.anglican.ca/assets/docs/The_Diaconate_Renewed_revised_March_2019.pdf>.

[4] I summarize this in *The Diaconate Renewed*, pp. 7–8.

[5] See ibid., pp. 9–11, 31–34.

[6] William T. Ditewig, *101 Questions and Answers on Deacons* (New York: Paulist Press, 2004), p. 22.

PART 1

The Theology of the Diaconate

CHAPTER 1

Theological Underpinnings of the Diaconate

Rosalind Brown

As we celebrate the ministry of deacons, which largely transcends our denominational and national specificities, my contribution on the theological underpinnings of diaconal ministry arises from some thinking that was prompted by John Collins' work as I asked Trinitarian questions of his helpful Christological contribution.

Underlying the truth at the heart of everything is our Christian identity as baptized Christians: what I describe as the "Russian-dolls" model of ordination, which reminds us that all ministry flows from who we are in Christ, not primarily from what we do. With Russian dolls, either on the outside we have a baptized Christian, inside some baptized Christians there is a deacon, inside some deacons there is a priest, and inside some priests there is a bishop; or we can look at it the other way round and say that at the heart of every vocation is a baptized Christian; some are called to diaconal ministry, some then wrap priestly ministry around it, and some are called to episcopal ministry, with priestly, diaconal, and baptismal ministry at its heart. Either way, we never cease being a baptized Christian and, if we are ordained, a deacon, and all vocations and ministries are interdependent and enable the ministry of all the baptized.

But we have to recognize that we've all been unsure at various stages in our respective histories just what or who a deacon is. I will focus on the Church of England, since it is easier to describe a particular situation. The 1662 *Book of Common Prayer* (BCP) Ordinal used hierarchical language when ordaining deacons to an "inferior office", understanding diaconal ministry as training for ordination to "higher" priestly ministry. That was the situation for centuries until 1980, when the Ordinal in the temporary *Alternative Service Book* removed the reference to the "inferior office". However, until 2000 and *Common Worship*, deacons were ordained for humble service, and there was still a reference to the possibility of future ordination as a priest. That has changed with *Common Worship*, as I will explain before asking what impact our new Ordinal has on our theology and understanding of the diaconate.

At the end of the twentieth century, the Church of England received John Collins' contribution to understanding diaconal ministry and embedded some of that in its Ordinal.[1] I will build on the now widely accepted Christological understanding and suggest complementing this with a more explicit pneumatological foundation for diaconal ministry as part of the proclamation of the kingdom of God.

In 2001, I was asked to chair a working party in the Diocese of Salisbury, which considered the scope for reviving the ministry of deacons, drawing on the recent national report, *For such a time as this*. Our report, *The Distinctive Diaconate*, was based on the new draft of the *Common Worship* Ordinal issued in 2000. *Common Worship* moved things on theologically by defining deacons as "ambassadors and heralds of Christ's kingdom". We welcomed this, but unfortunately the concept of ambassadorship did not survive into the final version of the *Common Worship* Ordinal in 2005.[2] I feel this is a loss, because heralds announce a message entrusted to them, but they do not carry the authority of an ambassador who represents, interprets, and responds on behalf of his or her commissioning authority. Interestingly, the Anglican Church of Australia describes deacons as "ambassadors" but not "heralds".

Common Worship makes the diaconate a full ministry in its own right, removing references to the possibility of future priestly ordination. Influenced by Collins, it models diaconal ministry on the example of Jesus Christ, rather than on Stephen as in the BCP. The ordination prayer now includes an invocation of the Holy Spirit. These significant reinterpretations of the diaconate have gone largely unremarked; it is not widely recognized that we are in new territory, which is why I think there are still residual misunderstandings based on centuries of the BCP

Ordinal: we are still in a time of transition with people ordained under both the old and new understandings of diaconal ministry.

The Revd Canon Joe Cassidy, speaking to the Diaconal Association of the Church of England in 2006, reflected on Acts 6; whilst recognizing that the men there are not named as deacons, he asked why the Church laid hands on them:

> . . .why ordain? . . . Why make such a formal fuss? . . . It seems to me that they formalised it because such service cuts to the heart of the Gospel, to the heart of what it means to be Church. . . . They evidently saw this sort of service as being central to the life of the emerging community. Hence the emphasis on the 'deacons' being filled with the Holy Spirit. The work of service was central to what the Holy Spirit was doing in that community.[3]

So what of us today? What is the Holy Spirit doing among us? What is the vision of the kingdom of God that drives the Church's ministry today? What animates and galvanizes the Church's ministry? What so electrifies the people of God that we cannot help but proclaim the good news of the coming of the kingdom of God? And where do deacons fit into this?

Theologically, within the broader context that the world is created, sustained and loved by God, all Christian ministry and engagement with the world flows from the incarnation, when God in Jesus Christ shared our life. Only then could he redeem us. Before Trinitarian theology developed, Ignatius perceived bishops as representing the Father, whereas deacons represented and were entrusted with the business of Jesus Christ.[4] Developing this, Bishop David Stancliffe wrote in the preface to the Salisbury Report on the Distinctive Diaconate:

> The Incarnation is the foundation of God's redeeming activity. It comes first. "That which God did not assume, he did not redeem", says Gregory of Nazianzus, making it clear that for God to change people, he needed first to engage with us and share human life. In the same way, the ministry of the deacon is the foundation of all ordained ministry. . . . The deacon focuses this sense of God sharing our life and engaging with us directly by making

God's incarnation, his being rooted in human life, central to the Church.[5]

Just as there had to be Jesus' incarnation before his resurrection, ascension, and sending of the Holy Spirit, so David Stancliffe argues, there must be incarnational engagement with the world before there can be transformative engagement. Deacons are ordained as visible signs and foci of the Church's vocation—that of all the baptized—to live the mission of God through deep, incarnational, life-giving engagement in the world today. Stancliffe adds that transformative ministry bringing resurrection new life is expressed in the sacramental ministry of the priest, while episcopal ministry, especially as exercised in confirmation and ordination, continues the sanctifying and empowering work of the Holy Spirit whom Jesus Christ sent on the Church after his ascension. And all ordained ministry is to enable all the baptized people of God to continue Christ's work in the world. Hence the Church of England's Ordinal describes deacons as being ordained so that the people of God may be better equipped to make Christ known.

John Collins drew on meanings of *diakonos* in early secular society to present the deacon as ambassador, attending to and entrusted with the business of Jesus Christ, a person on mission, a messenger, making connections, building bridges, faithfully delivering his or her mandate. This is far from an "inferior office". Paul understood himself as a *diakonos* with the Lord's commission (Romans 1:1), set apart for the gospel. In practice, Collins describes this as a call to share in Christ's servant ministry. So who is being served? A servant serves and obeys their master, not the recipient of that service. Paula Gooder provides the helpful contemporary example of a waiter in a restaurant whose job description requires him or her to serve customers well; waiters do not care for customers because they are kind (although that helps) but because their boss requires them to do so. Gooder concludes: "Service is more about carrying out orders than it is about looking after others."[6] The Faith and Order Advisory Group of the Church of England summed it up: "Collins' proposal changes the focus from what is done (i.e. humble service) to for whom it is done (i.e. who sends the *diakonos*)."[7] Kind actions express our service to God, and humans are the beneficiaries. Jesus' parable about the sheep and the goats comes to mind (Matthew 25:40, 45).

However, it seems that quite early on in the Church's history Ignatius had to correct an undue narrowing of the ministry of deacons, saying that they are not primarily deacons of meats and drinks; that was subsumed into their primary, Christ-centred, Spirit-empowered proclamation of the good news in word and deed. So, in Acts 6, Stephen performed signs, wonders, and prophetic proclamation and Philip was an evangelist (Acts 6:8–14; 8:26–40). This so destabilized the status quo that Stephen was martyred: as someone has commented, you are not martyred for serving food to elderly ladies. There was much more to their ministry than that and we should recover that perspective, as Ignatius did.

If deacons are about the business of Jesus, then that means being empowered and guided by the same Spirit who was involved in Jesus' conception, life, ministry and commissioning of others to proclaim the good news of the proximity of the kingdom of God (Mark 1:14–15; Luke 1:35; 2:25–35; 3:21–22; 4:1–2; 4:14–18; 24:48–49; Matthew 28:19–20; John 20:21–22), whom Jesus sent to equip the Church to share in his mission, culminating in his bestowal of the Holy Spirit on his apostles when sending them to proclaim the good news. Hence the apostles were looking for people not only of good standing and wisdom, but also full of the Spirit (Acts 6:3). The Spirit works through humans (Micah 3:8; 6:8). Pharaoh recognized the Spirit at work in Joseph (Genesis 41:38), Moses was assisted by men with whom the Spirit of God was shared (Numbers 11:17), and the Spirit empowered Isaiah for his message of good news to the oppressed and the year of the Lord's favour (Isaiah 61:1–3).

There is an eschatological element in this work of the Spirit and, in an early contribution to the revived debate about the diaconate, Robert Hannaford and Christine Hall suggested that the diaconate is a sign of discontinuity, because God's kingdom is not of this world. "The full import of the diaconal ministry of charity is . . . lost unless it is also seen as a powerful sacramental focus for our faith in the new age of God breaking into the present."[8] The Doctrine Commission of the Church of England wrote that it is the Holy Spirit who works to bring about expressions of the kingdom of God in the world today, forming people who, made in the image of God and renewed by the Spirit of God, embody the kingdom of God.[9]

The bishop probes ordinands about their calling to diaconal ministry, since they proclaim the proximity of God's coming kingdom. As our ordinals now recognize, diaconal ministry depends upon the empowering of the Holy Spirit and the invocation, "Send down the Holy Spirit on your servant *N* for the office and work of a deacon in your Church", is vital. This contrasts with the 1662 Ordinal, which simply charged the deacon to "take . . . authority to execute the office of a Deacon in the Church of God" and made no reference to the Holy Spirit.

So, in the given context that the mission entrusted to the Church derives from Christ's example of proclaiming the proximity of the kingdom of God, of God's creative and redemptive love for the world and for justice and mercy, and given that the Holy Spirit descended on Jesus at his baptism and Jesus sent the Holy Spirit to empower his disciples after his ascension, I suggest that the Christological foundation and model of diaconal ministry must be strengthened by recognizing and drawing on an explicit, Spirit-based, pneumatological underpinning. This gives added impetus to the deacon's role in the Church's mission of proclaiming the kingdom of God.

The Church of England Ordinal says:

> Deacons are ordained so that the people of God may be better equipped to make Christ known. Theirs is a life of visible self-giving. Christ is the pattern of their calling and their commission; . . . [They] serve as heralds of Christ's kingdom. They are to proclaim the gospel in word and deed, as agents of God's purposes of love.[10]

This is no "inferior office".

During discussions in Salisbury, someone suggested the language of deacon-missioner to encourage this ministry, particularly among evangelical and charismatic parishes. This reclaims the exemplar in Acts and aligns it clearly with the Five Marks of Mission which frame the ministry of the Anglican Church:

- To proclaim the Good News of the Kingdom;
- To teach, baptize and nurture new believers;
- To respond to human need by loving service;
- To seek to transform unjust structures of society, to challenge violence of every kind and to pursue peace and reconciliation;
- To strive to safeguard the integrity of creation and sustain and renew the life of the earth.[11]

These marks of mission rest on the redemption secured in Jesus Christ and his example of Spirit-empowered proclamation of the proximity of the kingdom of God. Without the stimulus and power of the Holy Spirit there would have been no spreading from Jerusalem and no fulfilment of this ministry today.

The Holy Spirit brings life where there is death. Focusing briefly on the fourth and fifth marks of mission, Isaiah describes people who are enlivened by God's Spirit as oaks of righteousness who rebuild ancient ruins, raise up former devastation and repair ruined cities and the devastations of many generations (Isaiah 61:3–4). Increasingly, deacons see their ministry as embodying and encouraging others in the care of God's creation, repairing "the devastations of many generations", whether ecological or urban. This deeply incarnational ministry reflects the mandate to tend the world (Genesis 1:28–31; 2:15–17). Pope Francis has written:

> We were not meant to be inundated by cement, asphalt, glass and metal, and deprived of physical contact with nature.... [A] true ecological approach always becomes a social approach; it must integrate questions of justice in debates on the environment, so as to hear both the cry of the earth and the cry of the poor.[12]

Over a century ago, Canon Henry Scott Holland from St Paul's Cathedral in London, a city which had in living memory suffered a Big Stink after the sewers failed, said "the more you believe in the Incarnation, the more you care about drains". Deacons care about today's equivalents of drains.

If diaconal ministry is incarnational, modelled on Jesus Christ, empowered by the Holy Spirit, the Church should act decisively by seeking out more diaconal vocations. The Church of England was challenged in 2001:

> A renewed diaconate . . . operating as a catalyst for Christian discipleship, in the mission space between worship and the world, can help the Church to become more incarnational. . . . We have not been good at doing equal justice to these two vital movements of the Church's life: sending and gathering. The re-envisioned diaconate can help to hold them together.[13]

If my thesis is correct, that the Church must take seriously the Holy Spirit's inspiration and enabling of deacons, then we should allow deacons to reinvigorate the mission impetus of their ministry, facilitating and focusing Spirit-led mission in God's world. Incarnational diaconal ministry combines pastoral care of needy people with prophetic ministry in the world, speaking by word and action into situations of injustice or need, proclaiming the gospel in its fullness. This sits with the scripture's description of the Spirit's activity in creation, bringing life and renewal (Genesis 1:2, 2:7; Psalm 104:30), righteous judgement of the poor, peace, wholeness and joy, justice and light for the nations, care for the vulnerable, liberty for captives (Isaiah 11:12, 42).

I suggested in *Being a Deacon Today* that the deacon belongs in three places: the Church, the world and the margins,[14] those far margins of the world among people who never set foot in church, because its doorstep is a hard-to-cross threshold into an unfamiliar world. From this flows the diaconal mandate to bring the needs of the world to the attention of the Church in the intercessions and to send people out to help to meet those needs. Diaconal ministry is a dynamic extension of eucharistic celebration, as deacons are incarnational ministers of the Eucharist in the forgotten, awkward corners of the world. So they should be freed to be busy on those margins with the lonely, the overlooked, the homeless, and the misfits; to be the eucharistic Church present and active, challenging societal injustices from a theological and practical perspective.

For example, food banks began with Christians in Salisbury, coordinated by a Roman Catholic deacon, and we expect to find deacons in asylum centres, prisons, debt advice centres, as Street Pastors,[15] and in other forms of engagement which address the contemporary equivalents of the needs Isaiah envisaged being met by the Spirit's inspiration. This distinctively diaconal ministry is distinguished from equally vital professional or voluntary work, because deacons are the Church's ordained and representative people who integrate the practical care of the needy beyond the doors of the church back to the church in prophetic and challenging ways, leading the church in response. Deacons are evangelists for mission. A deacon commissioned to be the bishop's representative could enable the ministry of, or be a resource for, several parishes by providing practical leadership on the ground and bringing the needs encountered there to the bishop and churches for prayer and response.

There is always a danger of confusing ordination with clericalism, a travesty Pope Francis describes as making people feel discarded or abused. As a world, we have lost sight of leadership that assists, models, and empowers rather than being in the limelight. Deacons are ordained to set a virtuous circle in motion by enabling and resourcing the ministry of all baptized Christians, wherever they live and work. It is different leadership from that of the priest or bishop, but it is leadership nonetheless, modelled on Christ's example and empowered by the Holy Spirit, making and maintaining the connections between church and world, transforming situations, keeping the mission of God before the Church. This could revolutionize the mission of the Church. Joe Cassidy dreamed aloud:

> What if each of our parishes had seven or so deacons, charged not just with maintaining and leading liturgy in the community, but chiefly that ensuring justice was done and that justice issues were addressed? . . . What if every Bishop had seven deacons assigned to him or her; deacons who spent their time on the lookout for ways in which our communal lives might be subverting the apostolic work of the Church? . . . What would our presbyters and bishops sound like were they thus empowered to preach from a platform marked by more integrity? Can you imagine a Church where priests and bishops were emboldened by a Church that sacrificially cared for others? Can you imagine how differently they might preach?[16]

Francis of Assisi is famously reported to have told his followers to proclaim the gospel and use words if they needed to. The privilege of diaconal ministry is to be entrusted with the business of Jesus Christ. And, as St John tells us, "the Word became flesh and dwelt among us, and we have seen his glory, the glory as of a Father's only Son, full of grace and truth" (John 1:14). For the privilege of being about the business of Jesus Christ in the world, thanks be to God.

Notes

[1]   Collins' work has been described by Paul Avis as "having a seismic effect on the understanding of diaconal ministry" (Paul Avis, *A Ministry Shaped by Mission*, London: T & T Clark, 2005), p. 105.

[2]   Published in 2007 as The Church of England, *The Ordination of Deacons* (London: Church House Publishing, 2007), available at <https://www.church ofengland.org/prayer-and-worship/worship-texts-and-resources/common-worship/ministry/common-worship-ordination-services#mm012>, accessed frequently, most recently 2 January 2016.

[3]   Joseph Cassidy, "The Renewed Diaconate", paper given at the AGM of the Diaconal Association of the Church of England, 4 February 2006. I am grateful to Roy Overthrow for providing me with a copy.

[4]   Ignatius, *Epistle to the Trallians* 2:3–3:1, and *Epistle to the Magnesians* 6:1.

[5]   David Stancliffe, in Diocese of Salisbury, *The Distinctive Diaconate* (Salisbury: Sarum College Press, 2003), p. 6.

[6]   Paula Gooder, "Diakonia in the New Testament: A Dialogue with John Collins. Porvoo Consultation 2006", *Ecclesiology* 3:1, pp. 33–56.

[7]   The Faith and Order Advisory Group of the Church of England, *The Mission and Ministry of the Whole Church*, 2007, p. 23.

[8]   Robert Hannaford, "Towards a Theology of the Diaconate", in Christine Hall (ed.), *The Deacon's Ministry* (Leominster: Gracewing, 1991), pp. 38–39.

[9]   The Doctrine Commission of the Church of England, *We Believe in the Holy Spirit* (London: Central Board of Finance of the Church of England, 1993), p. 60.

[10] The Church of England, op cit., p. 2007.

11 The Five Marks of Mission were developed by the Anglican Consultative Council between 1984 and 2012 and adopted by the General Synod of the Church of England in 1996. They can be found at <https://www.churchof england.org/media/1918854/the%20five%20marks%20of%20mission.pdf>.

12 *Encyclical Letter 'Laudato Si' of the Holy Father Francis on Care for our Common Home,* 2015, <http://cafod.org.uk/content/download/25373/182331 /file/papa-francesco_20150524_enciclica-laudato-si_en.pdf>, accessed 21 January 2016, paragraphs 44 and 49.

13 Church of England House of Bishops, *For such a time as this* (London: Church House Publishing, 2001), p. 30.

14 Rosalind Brown, *Being a Deacon Today* (Norwich: Canterbury Press, 2005).

15 In the United Kingdom, Street Pastors are church members who go out on city streets all night on Fridays and Saturdays to assist party-goers who are in need of immediate practical care and help, usually as a result of drink or drugs. There is a role for deacons in enabling and coordinating this ministry.

16 Cassidy, op cit.

CHAPTER 2

The Deacon and Sacramental Character

Frederick C. Bauerschmidt

Even now, some fifty years after the official restoration in the Roman Catholic Church of the diaconate as a permanent and not merely transitional ordained ministry (Paul VI, *Sacrum diaconatus ordinem*, 18 June 1967), deacons frequently find themselves in the position of having to explain what a deacon is. This is usually done in response to questions that, roughly speaking, take one of two forms: (a) how does a deacon differ from a priest? and (b) how does a deacon differ from a lay person?

This, I would argue, puts the deacon in a difficult situation, theologically speaking, not simply because it defines the deacon in terms of what a deacon is not, but also because it tends to define the deacon in terms of "power": the deacon differs from the priest, because the deacon lacks the power to celebrate the Eucharist, hear confessions, and anoint the sick; the deacon differs from the lay person, because the deacon has the power to . . .—well, here we run into more difficulty, because there is precious little that a deacon can do that, under certain circumstances and with special delegation, a lay person cannot do. Deacons, but not lay people, are allowed to give the greeting "The Lord be with you" in the liturgy, can give Eucharistic Benediction with the monstrance, and can bless certain things such as water, religious medals and rosaries. That's really about it. With proper permission, a lay person can baptize, preside at weddings, preach (outside the context of the Eucharist), give Communion, and do many of the things that might be seen as candidates for the "powers" of the deacon. Furthermore, both priests and lay people, and not only deacons, can and must engage in the ministry of charity and service to those in need that is sometimes seen as the hallmark of the diaconate. So, what is a deacon?

All of this has suggested to some that thinking of the diaconate in terms of "powers" conferred by diaconal ordination might not be the best way to approach the matter. It is increasingly said, to the point where it is becoming something of a cliché, that the diaconate is first and foremost about "being" and not about "doing": it is about being an icon of Christ, who came to serve and not be served. And it is from this "being" that the "doing" of diaconal ministry flows. And this is all true: as Thomas Aquinas teaches with regard to all beings, it is from the "first act", the act of existing, that all secondary acts—what we ordinarily think of as a thing's "activities"—flow (see, e.g., *De Potentia* q. 1 a. 1). A thing acts on the basis of how it exists. Rocks engage in rock-like activities, such as falling when dropped, because they exist in a rocky way; plants engage in plant-like activities, such as photosynthesis, because they exist in a plantish way; and human beings engage in human-like activities, such as coming up with the Pythagorean theorem or giving academic papers, because they exist in a human way. Likewise, we can say that deacons engage in deacon-like activities, such as service at the altar, the proclamation of the Word and the ministry of charity, because they exist in a diaconal way—that is, as an icon of Christ the servant.

Yet, as true as this all is, I am not sure it really helps in explaining to inquirers what a deacon is. Am I really more of an icon of Christ the servant than Teresa of Calcutta or Dorothy Day? Clearly, the difference between a deacon and someone else who presents us with an image of Christ the servant is that the deacon is *ordained* to this role; the *being* of the deacon is somehow configured to Christ as servant through the rite of ordination, which, prior to any notion of "powers" conferred, is about entry into a particular "order"—the order of deacons. This order occupies a particular space within the ordering of Christ's body, that ordering that we call "hierarchy", and in coming to occupy this space the deacon takes on a new existential quality. The traditional way of expressing this is to say that ordination to the diaconate confers on a person a particular sacramental "character" or "seal" by which that person is configured to Christ, "who made himself the 'deacon' or servant of all" (*Catechism of the Catholic Church*, n. 1570).

Drawing on both Augustine's reflections on the unrepeatability of Christian baptism, along with Dionysius the Areopagite's theology of ecclesiastic hierarchy, the scholastics of the twelfth and thirteenth centuries began to speak of certain sacraments—baptism, confirmation and holy orders—as having as a part of their effect brought about *ex opere operato*, the bestowing of sacramental character. Sacramental character can be understood as an enduring disposition within the soul to a certain kind of activity—a kind of "second nature", not entirely unlike a moral virtue. Mark Jordan characterizes Thomas Aquinas' understanding of sacramental character as

> a principle or source of action rather than an inert product of some finished gesture. Character is a conferred role, not a written figure, no mark or stain. The role carries out actions that distinguish Christian life—and specifically, "worship of God according to Christian ritual" (3.63.1 ad 1; cf. 62.5 *corpus*).[1]

Sacramental character is our participation in the priesthood of Christ or, as we might say today, his threefold office of priest, prophet and ruler. In baptism we become worshippers of God, members of the liturgical assembly; in confirmation we become witnesses of the gospel to the world; in holy orders we become ministers within the body of Christ. Because character is a disposition to action, it encompasses both being and doing: it is an existential state that is associated with characteristic activities: worshipping, witnessing, ministering. Within the one sacrament of order, we find a distinction drawn between the priestly character of bishop and presbyter and the ministerial character of the deacon, such that we can speak of three distinct orders. As both Canon Law and the Catechism make clear, the sacramental character of the diaconate does not empower the deacon to act *in persona Christi Capitis* (in the person of Christ the Head), but gives rather the capacity "to serve the people of God in the *diaconia* [*sic!*] of liturgy, word and charity, in communion with the bishop and his presbyterate" (*Catechism of the Catholic Church*, n. 875).

To return to the notion of the deacon as an icon of Christ the servant, one might say that while Teresa of Calcutta or Dorothy Day were indeed living icons of Christ the servant, they were not this by virtue of having been sacramentally "located" in a particular place within the structure of the Church. They are not, as it were, icons *ex opere operato*, but rather charismatically, according to the free movement of the Spirit. A deacon, by virtue of the sacramental character of ordination, is irrevocably configured to Christ as servant. Deacons may, through indolence or indiscretion or garden-variety idiocy, prove to be poor icons of the one who came not to be served but to serve, but they retain their iconic status regardless, because their configuration to Christ grows not from their personal holiness, but from the public sacramental act of the Church locating them within the order of deacons.

Such a view presumes, obviously, that the sacrament of order "does something". Of course, everyone thinks that ordination does *something*, but the question is, how do we conceive of the something that it does? Even if we agree that the sacrament of order confers sacramental character, what exactly does that mean? Is this character the conferral of a disposition previously absent, or is it the sacramental recognition of a disposition already possessed, whether naturally or charismatically, now relocated into the heart of the Church?

On one model, the sacrament of order brings about a reality that was hitherto absent; it grants spiritual gifts and powers that, whilst not magically guaranteeing that the ordinand will be a rousing diaconal success, bring about a new state of being. This approach, which sees ordination as a bestowal of grace, is perhaps reflected in the Second Vatican Council's Dogmatic Constitution on the Church, *Lumen gentium*, in a statement concerning the diaconate: "strengthened by sacramental grace, they are at the service of the people of God in the ministry of the liturgy, the word and charity" (*Lumen gentium* 29).

On another model, the sacrament of order serves to name and ratify a diaconal reality already inchoately present. This view, which sees ordination as an affirmation of a gift already given, is perhaps reflected in Vatican II's Decree on the Missionary Activity of the Church, *Ad gentes*, which states, "It would be helpful to those men who are exercising what is in fact the ministry of deacon . . . to be strengthened, and bound more closely to the altar, by the imposition of hands which has come down from the apostles, so that they may be able to carry out their ministry more effectively through the sacramental grace of the diaconate" (*Ad gentes* 16).

I do not want to oversell the difference between two documents issuing from the same ecumenical council. *Ad gentes* does speak of the working of sacramental grace, given through ordination, in the life of the deacon. However, it seems to presume that there is a diaconal ministry already present and active that is not so much conferred by the sacrament as it is strengthened and given a liturgical component. *Lumen gentium*, on the other hand, while similarly speaking of the strengthening power of sacramental grace, seems to presume that diaconal ministry in its true sense is not yet present until sacramentally conferred. What we might call the *Ad gentes* model underscores the continuity between the pre- and post-ordination identity of the deacon, while what we might call the *Lumen gentium* model emphasizes the novelty of the reality brought about by the sacrament of order.

My general impression is that the *Ad gentes* model has been somewhat favoured in the decades since the Second Vatican Council over the *Lumen gentium* model. These two models have certain implications for how we think of diaconal ministry that I would like to spell out, and in the course of spelling them out, I would like to argue, swimming somewhat against the tide, that the *Lumen gentium* model, if not wholly superior to the *Ad gentes* model, has certain features that might commend it to us.

First, the *Ad gentes* model, stressing continuity, would suggest that in discerning diaconal vocations we should look toward those who are already exercising, to quote the Council, "what is in fact the ministry of deacon." This of course presumes that we have a clear idea of what diaconal ministry is, that we can itemize its features. And for a while there did seem to be a consensus that the ministry of deacon was the ministry of humble, even menial, service: serving in soup kitchens, visiting the sick and imprisoned, and so forth. This consensus was the view of many, if not all, of those who called for the restoration of the permanent diaconate in the 1940s and 50s and remains the view held by a large number of people today. As Edward P. Echlin wrote in 1971, "In pre-Christian literature, including the Septuagint version of the Old Testament, *diakonos, diakoein* and *diakonia* referred to service, especially the menial service of assistance at tables."[2] While liturgical ministry might be the most visible activity of deacons, it is often said that the liturgical ministry of the deacon is a subsidiary ministry to the ministry of charity. And there are good reasons behind this view; even apart from the Seven in the Book of Acts who were set apart to "serve at tables", caring for the Hellenist widows, we have stories of deacons like Lawrence, who, in addition to maintaining his courage and sense of humour whilst being roasted on a grill, was given charge over the church of Rome's ministry to the poor, or Francis of Assisi, who remained a deacon his whole life and was particularly devoted to poverty and simplicity.

Yet, without denying that the diaconate has the ministry of charity as an integral element, the work of John N. Collins has called into question the notion that *diakonia* in the New Testament always means menial service.[3] Collins argues that if we actually look at the use of the term in both biblical and extra-biblical literature, it indicates not humility but rather acting on behalf of and at the behest of another. A deacon is not simply anyone who engages in humble service, but rather precisely that person who has been commissioned and sent by Christ to represent him. If Collins is right, then the *Ad gentes* model of ordination as a ratification of "what is in fact the ministry of deacon" faces not only the question of what the ministry of deacon is, but also that of how we can have diaconal ministry present prior to Christ's sacramental act of calling and sending. The *Lumen gentium* model of ordination as founding and establishing diaconal identity and ministry perhaps fits better with this emerging understanding of what the New Testament means by *diakonia* as fulfilling a mandate received from a higher authority. Here, one truly *becomes* a deacon through the sacrament of order, because it is here that one receives the mandate of Christ, through the instrumental action of the bishop.

This view helps make sense of the historic relationship between the deacon and the bishop. The deacon's status as one sent by Jesus Christ is sacramentalized through his relationship with the bishop. The deacon differs from the presbyter by having a direct mandate from the bishop (signified ritually in the Roman Rite by the bishop alone laying hands on the deacon), not one mediated by the collegial relationships of the presbyterate (signified ritually by the presbyters joining the bishop in laying hands on the one to be ordained to the priesthood).

This freeing of *diakonia* from a monolithic model of menial service also has practical implications for discerning diaconal vocations. Perhaps we ought not look only to those who have a proven track record of humble service; perhaps there might be a place for diaconal assertiveness, if not diaconal presidency. Whilst acknowledging the historic example of humble deacons, we ought to take account of the full range of ways in which those ordained to the diaconate have functioned in the history of the Church. Lawrence was in fact a fairly powerful figure, controlling as he did much of the assets of the Roman Church; the diaconate was flexible enough to include not just humble Francis of Assisi, but also a hymn writer like Ephraem and a scholar like Alcuin.

Second, the *Ad gentes* model of diaconal ordination as a ratification of those already engaged in "what is in fact the ministry of deacon" might seem to suggest that the diaconate has a monopoly on *diakonia*, since it seems to assimilate the *diakonia* of the laity to the ordained diaconate. If a Christian who is devoted to service is already, to borrow a term from Karl Rahner, an "anonymous deacon",[4] only awaiting public ratification via ordination, then how can we understand the call to imitate Christ as servant to be an imperative rooted in baptism, something that one might be called to without being called to ordination? It would be as if we treated anyone who offered prayer to God as an "anonymous priest" awaiting ratification of their priesthood via ordination to the presbyterate. If, however, ordination creates not simply *diakonia*, but the *ministry* of *diakonia*, the identity of one who acts upon a mandate from a higher authority through admission to the order of deacons, then we can perhaps get a purchase on how deacons in their ministry differ from the laity who also live as icons of Christ the servant.

Indeed, I would suggest that just as there is a distinction between the baptismal priesthood of the faithful and the ministerial priesthood of presbyters and bishops, both of which are participations in the one priesthood of Christ (*Catechism of the Catholic Church*, n. 1546), so too a distinction can be made between the baptismal *diakonia* of the faithful and the ministerial *diakonia* of deacons. Just as the ministerial priesthood is "at the service of the common priesthood . . . directed at the unfolding of the baptismal grace of all Christians" (*Catechism of the Catholic Church*, n. 1547), so too the ministerial *diakonia* is at the service of the common *diakonia* and directed to the unfolding for the faithful the diaconal heart of their identity as Christians. The deacon, mandated by the *episkopos*, who has oversight of the wellbeing of the local church as a whole, should animate and assist the *diakonia* that the faithful live out in their everyday lives. And deacons do this not simply by their particular activities, but by their very identity, their sacramental setting-apart as icons of Christ. As Paul McPartlan puts it, "deacons are, in fact, *signs* to the church of what *all* in the church should be doing".[5]

One way to say this would be to say that deacons serve within the Church so that the faithful may carry out their own participation in the priestly, prophetic and royal office of Christ, by offering fitting worship to God and bearing witness to Christ in the world. The sacramental character of order is a disposition to an *ad intra* activity, which has as its goal both the *ad intra* worship and the *ad extra* witness of the entire people of God.

Of course, this language of *ad intra* and *ad extra* raises another set of questions. Is this too simple a division of labour: can our activities really be divided up into the intra-ecclesial and the extra-ecclesial? Does the deacon as deacon (rather than simply as a member of the faithful) have an *ad extra* ministry? How are deacons understood vis-à-vis lay people who also minister *within* the Church, often lay women for whom, in a Roman Catholic context, ordination is not an option? But these might not be questions we can settle here.

Notes

[1]   Mark Jordan, "Sacramental Characters", *Studies in Christian Ethics* 19:6 (2006), p. 327.

[2]   Edward P. Echlin, *The Deacon in the Church: Past and Future* (New York: Alba House, 1971), pp. 4–5.

[3]   See, for example, the essays in *Diakonia Studies: Critical Issues in Ministry* (Oxford: Oxford University Press, 2014).

[4]   Karl Rahner, "The Theology of the Restoration of the Diaconate", in *Theological Investigations V: Later Writings* (London: Darton, Longman & Todd Ltd., 1966), pp. 277–278.

[5] "The Deacon and *Gaudium et Spes*", in James Keating (ed.), *The Deacon Reader* (New York: Paulist Press, 2006), p. 70.

PART 2

The Transitional Diaconate in Question

CHAPTER 3

The Conundrum of the
Transitional Diaconate

Susanne Watson Epting

If only most of the conundrums that we face today were as minor as that of the transitional diaconate! While there was a time when many of us devoted great energy in seeking to influence the Episcopal Church, the greater conundrum in this time we live in is a larger question about the Church's continued relevance in a world that is itself a conundrum.

Over twenty years ago, the North American Association for the Diaconate, now known as the Association for Episcopal Deacons, published a small collection of papers in a slim volume called *The Orders of Ministry: Reflections on Direct Ordination, 1996*. In the introduction to that little book,[1] the Revd Dr John Docker, who was then head of the Episcopal Church Office for Ministry Development, explained that for many years there had been General Convention resolutions asking for a canonical change that would enable persons to "be ordained to the order to which the church [had] called them, without passing through another order".[2] In fact, in 1991, the General Convention of the Episcopal Church adopted a resolution directing the Theology Committee of the House of Bishops to prepare a paper on direct ordination. During the next triennium, the Council on the Development of Ministry, under the oversight of John Docker, looked at the pros and cons of direct ordination. The volume that the North American Association produced was with their help and contained several pro and con articles.

The paper commissioned for the House of Bishops was written by the Revd Dr Louis Weil and was entitled "Should the Episcopal Church

Permit Direct Ordination?" That paper will serve here, at least in part, as a starting place for these remarks. There are two reasons for that. The first is that Professor Weil has, for decades, been one scholar we can count on to consider vocation in the context of all the baptized. That is, rather than comparing one order to another, our common baptismal identity is his starting place. Secondly, while acknowledging the different understandings and patterns of ordination throughout history, he reminds us that even though direct ordinations did take place in our history, and sequential ordination was slow to develop, "we cannot choose an ideal in the past, lift it out of its historical framework, whether patristic, medieval or Reformation, and impose it on our situation in the present" . . . but "our deliberation . . . must take many factors into account . . . ."[3]

Part of the conundrum, then, is to decide just what factors should be taken into account. In the contemporary Episcopal Church, there are two especially identifiable arguments against direct ordination. The first is that which embraces the pattern of medieval society, in which the Church allowed itself to be enculturated and was thus drawn into a hierarchical model of authority that included a very complicated system of major and minor orders. One needed to "ascend the ladder", so to speak, and demonstrate one's skills and talents in each stage. Thus, even after Thomas Cranmer abolished the minor orders, the sequential model remained, partly with the idea of each order being a training ground for another. A second argument against direct ordination has been that the basis of all ordained ministry is service. This perception presumes that ordination to the diaconate somehow legitimizes the call to service, thus confusing (if not diminishing) our call to service at baptism.

However, as we consider those arguments at this point in our history in the Episcopal Church, I believe there are some factors to consider that have to do with longevity, in both contemporary history and practice, that address both of those arguments. The current version of the *Book of Common Prayer* in the Episcopal Church has officially been in use for forty years. While forty years can seem a short time in the long history of the Church, it is important to recognize that we are continuing to make history—indeed we are a part of history, and there are lessons we can learn from emerging patterns. The current Episcopal Prayer Book is important as we examine the "conundrum of the transitional diaconate".

One of the shifts that occurred in the 1979 Prayer Book was in the ordination rite for deacons. In the previous version of 1928, deacons were described as an "inferior order" and served a period during which they were to show they were "worthy to be called unto the higher Ministries . . . ".[4] However, in the 1979 Prayer Book, the language of inferiority was removed, as was any reference to proving oneself worthy to a "higher" order. In fact, Louis Weil reminds us in his essay that "[t]here is clearly here a significant shift of focus which must be linked to the introductory rubric at the Ordination of a Priest, and which states that 'The ordinand is to be vested in surplice or alb, without stole, tippet or other vesture distinctive of ecclesiastical or academic rank or order'". He goes on, "in other words, the rites suggest in these texts a recovery of a sense of the theological integrity of each order . . . ."

His endnotes refer us to studies published during the preparatory stages of the 1979 Prayer Book, where we read, "Each order is presented as a distinctive vocation, having its own characteristics. This avoids the misleading impression that the three orders are simply in an ascending scale of promotions."[5] These notes were published nearly ten years before the official use of the 1979 book occurred. It is important to acknowledge that what came with the revised version of the Prayer Book had been studied for some time, so when the book was finally adopted, it was as the result of these studies and significant trial use. This addresses, at least in part, the argument about sequential ordination.

However, there is something much more significant about the context in which the rites were changed. That is that baptism was reclaimed as full initiation, that it should be public, that it is incorporation into the larger body of Christ, and that it is as significant to the community as it is to the individual being baptized. With that shift in the baptismal rite came a deeper understanding that the first call to ministry is at baptism, that we all have gifts to offer, and that ministry is not something owned by clergy, or something that we do to each other, but is our common call. Ministry, then, whether ordained, specialized, that in daily life—all is held with baptism as the primary identity. Of course, we are all called to service at our baptism.

At the same time a renewed vision of the diaconate was set forward, so with the 1979 *Book of Common Prayer* we see the old arguments about inferior order and apprenticeship being diminished in practice. With the renewal of the centrality of baptism and a renewed vision of the diaconate, we see the move toward not just a diaconate that has to do service performed by particular individuals, but one that points toward the *diakonia* of all the baptized and a servant *church*. In my own book, *Unexpected Consequences: The Diaconate Renewed*, I trace the evolution and strong identity of our contemporary diaconate. In the Episcopal Church today, there should be no question about the meaning or purpose of the Order of Deacons. Most of the three thousand deacons in the Episcopal Church have been ordained from the rites in the 1979 Prayer Book, with this renewed understanding of both baptism and ordination.

In addition, for nearly fifty years, the canons of the Episcopal Church have mandated the existence of Commissions on Ministry in each diocese. They provide advice and oversight to bishops regarding those called to ordination. They ensure that the canons that guide the ordination process are followed and competencies assessed. Indeed, those aspiring to holy orders are tracked and measured and tested. By 2003, the canons of the Episcopal Church had been changed in ways that clearly differentiated the type of training necessary for deacons and presbyters, thus acknowledging the more distinctive nature of each order. What then does a six-month probationary period as a transitional deacon do for anyone? For those of us who have lived this vocation for years, it is hard not to bristle when those who have served as a deacon for six months think they understand all there is to know about being a deacon. I daresay none of us would presume to say we know what it is like to be a presbyter or a bishop, even though we may exercise ministry in our lives that has to do with reconciliation or oversight.

Then why this conundrum? I would like to suggest some possible answers and ask some questions for further exploration and discussion. In fact, I might rename all this as "the conundrum of the presbyterate" for a start. For some forty years, at least in the Episcopal Church, we have studied the diaconate. We have defined and rehearsed. We have strengthened our education and formation programmes. We have regularly reviewed and modified them. We have claimed who we are and who the Church asks us to be. We have claimed who we are especially in relation to baptism and the larger body of Christ. However, as times have changed, and our rites have changed, and our ecclesiology has changed, we have not examined the presbyterate in the same way.

Most people think they have a very good knowledge of what a presbyter is. And yet it was very telling one day when I was in a discussion with some presbyters who were struggling with an interesting identity question. A couple of them were frustrated and longing for a place to talk about what it means to be a priest, rather than a rector. Is it possible that there is something about the role of a rector that keeps us tied to sequence and hierarchy, rather than charism and sacramental call?

The question has also been raised as the Church has looked for alternative models of training for presbyters. Local formation programmes show us that not everyone has to go away to seminary. That change has met with both positive and negative responses. In some places locally trained presbyters have been looked on as second-class. In other places, they have been embraced. What is at the core of this variety of responses? Presbyters have not been called upon in quite the same intentional way to look at who they are in relationship to baptism. In fact, one of the many contributors to the 1979 BCP suggested that "one of the major contributions of the book was to address the problem of clericalism". Again, this was done not just through some changes in the ordination rites, but in the deep significance and reminder that baptism, rather than ordination, is the most important event in the life of a Christian.[6]

What else might we need to address in further considering this conundrum? I would suggest that we might well be stuck in the sentimental rather than the logical, and that a re-examination of the *theological* is more important than the historical. What do I mean when I say that we might be stuck in the sentimental rather than the logical? Anecdotal evidence suggests to me that there is often a sentimental or emotional attachment to the diaconate, for those who would argue to keep sequential orders. Some presbyters are convinced that ordination to the diaconate, rather than the call to service at baptism, serves as the foundation for holy orders. They tend to be the same clergy who, in order to remind themselves and others of a kind of "servant status", would find it more important for clergy to wash the feet of the congregation, rather than have the congregation participate in that ritual with each other. In this scenario, we highlight the role of the ordained, potentially diminishing the call to all of God's people to serve.

As more and more people in our church see a strong and renewed diaconate, they realize the difference in the gifts and training necessary for the distinctive orders. In addition, some presbyters are very clear that they are bothered by having to answer, in their ordination to the transitional diaconate, whether they feel truly called to be a deacon. People in our congregations have come to understand the renewed diaconate more clearly and are quite clear on the distinctive roles of deacons and priests.

I would like to suggest, then, that re-examining the theological is more important than further rehearsing historical patterns and precedents of hierarchy and sequence. Just what does ordination mean in relationship to baptism? What does it mean to live as the body of Christ that claims baptism as the first call to ministry? At the risk of asking something scandalous, what do we mean by servanthood? We acknowledge the importance of the servant nature of Christ, but how do we recognize the servant nature of Christ's Church? In our dominant-culture-defined Church, how many church leaders truly understand what it is to be a servant? I daresay the word means something different to an African-American woman living in the southern United States than it does to the privileged white person kneeling to be ordained as a transitional deacon. I suspect that the word means something different to all of those who have been "in service", living their own kind of obedience to the wealthiest in our cultures who employ them.

I believe we should tread very carefully in using that "servant" word. We are, after all, talking about not just the image of Jesus with the basin and the towel, but the grave responsibility and authority that come with it. It is about the willingness to count the cost of living a life that calls us to challenge the powers, bring hope to the poor, and enter life's wounds, working for justice and healing and reconciliation. There are skills to be developed in both individuals and communities, training to do these things themselves that cannot be taken lightly. For those who spend years developing these skills, skills that clearly help define and empower diaconal ministry, it is clear that such preparation is distinct from that of our friends who are called to gather the community and preside at the altar.

Finally, in order to put the conundrum of the transitional diaconate into a larger context, that which has to do with the Church's continued relevance in a world that is itself a conundrum, I would ask:

> How does the transitional diaconate strengthen the Church?

If we remain slow to change our canons to eliminate sequential ordination, what changes might we make to the ordination rites? Might a renewal of our baptismal vows serve to reground us in the first call to ministry? Might there be different ordination rites for transitional deacons?

> Finally, how does the transitional diaconate contribute to the Church's mission and witness?

In the end, holy orders do not exist for their own sake.

> The diaconate does not exist for the sake of having deacons, but for the sake of reaching out in the wholesome humility of Christ, making the Church relevant, making the world whole. Nor does the presbyterate exist for the sake of immovable altars and fonts, but for the sake of breaking the bread in daily life and of keeping the community together as we move away from privilege. Nor does the episcopate exist for the sake of churchly order, but for the sake of a deeper unity that is unafraid to question its effectiveness, insisting that it be a unity that undergirds the mission and ministry of the whole people of God.[7]

What then is our conundrum?

Notes

1.   Edwin F. Hallenbeck (ed.), *The Orders of Ministry, Reflections on Direct Ordination, 1996* (Providence, RI: North American Association for the Diaconate, 1996).

2.   Ibid., p. ix.

3.   Ibid., p. 56.

4.   BCP, 1928, p. 535.

5.   *The Orders of Ministry: Reflections on Direct Ordination, 1996*, pp. 54 and 64.

6.   Susanne Watson Epting, *Unexpected Consequences: The Diaconate Renewed* (New York: Morehouse Publishing, 2015), pp. 40ff.

7.   Ibid., p. 172.

Integrity of Vocation and the Transitional Diaconate

Alison Peden

The Scottish Episcopal Church

The Scottish Episcopal Church (SEC) emerged at the Scottish Reformation of 1560, alongside the Presbyterian Church of Scotland. We are not "established", and we are very small—with just over three hundred and fifty congregations and about four hundred clergy. But we take our place in the Anglican Communion as one of the two provinces that do not owe their origin to the Church of England, the other being, of course, the Episcopal Church of the United States.

The theology of diaconal ministry was raised in 1987 in the SEC by a working group report entitled *Truly Called by God to Serve as a Deacon.*[1] This encouraged our Church to be fully involved in the consultations held by the Porvoo Communion in 2006 and 2009, and our Faith and Order Board set up a small group to respond to the recommendations issuing from these consultations. A further report (*Truly Called . . . 2*) was issued by this Diaconate Working Group in 2012.

Although there are only seven deacons in our Province, we now have four in training. This reflects two main developments: one is that we are very consciously rediscovering our vocation to mission in response to the real contemporary need in Scottish society. The strains of post-industrialism, prolonged governmental austerity, and uncertainty about our national and global identity have heightened social needs in Scottish society and made more urgent the Church's call to mission. The other driving force is the Principal of our Training Institute, Canon Anne Tomlinson, herself a deacon and one of the really significant advocates of the meaning and importance of the diaconal order. The Diaconate Working Group continues to develop our Province's thinking on the diaconate and to support the formation of our deacons. This paper emerges from the group, and its findings will be presented to the Faith and Order Board of the SEC for consideration.

In this chapter, I speak from a presbyteral point of view about the integrity of vocation and the sanctity of ordination. I am of the firm belief that our theology of the diaconate must develop within a broad theology of ministry that takes fully into account the various ways in which God calls us to build up the Church. I should be clear here that I am not presenting the agreed doctrine of the SEC in what I shall say, but the fruit of theological reflection on my own experience.

Introduction: Personal experience

Nearly twenty years ago, I began to articulate the vocation I sensed to be an Anglican priest and entered the discernment process of the SEC. I was assessed according to the Criteria for Selection of Priests by the Diocesan Director of Ordinands, the Provincial Director of Ordinands, a Provincial Advisory Panel, and a Bishops' Advisory Panel run by the Ministry Division of the Church of England (which the SEC used as part of the process). I entered training for priestly ministry, which included completing a MTh in Ministry, for some of which I was taught by Presbyterians and Baptists, to whom I had to explain my theology of priesthood, distinguishing it from diaconal ministry. I was offered a curacy in a congregation by the bishop, with the intention that I would train to be an incumbent priest. When we met to talk about ordination, I asked whether I could complete the first year as a probationary lay person and then be ordained as a priest, the calling that I and the Church had discerned had been given to me by God. My bishop rebuked me sharply and told me to go away and learn some humility.

I was bruised by this, because I had thought I *was* being humble. The study I had done about ministry had not only revealed to me the complexity and richness of different ministries, but had also shown me that I did not possess the charisms belonging to a deacon. For example, I had done some chaplaincy work in a women's prison in Scotland as part of my formation, and I really enjoyed leading a Bible study group there, preparing an inmate for confirmation, and gathering the women for worship. I knew I wasn't so good at connecting them with the right social care or protesting about the social conditions that had put them in prison in the first place. That is: I was better at using presbyteral gifts than diaconal ones.

As my study and formation progressed, I had become more aware of the diversity of the Holy Spirit's gifts to the body of Christ and their value and dignity. I read *Baptism, Eucharist and Ministry*[2] and the theologies of ministry that explored diaconate, priesthood and episcopacy as different *dimensions* of service rather than different *rungs in a hierarchy*.[3] Being required to be ordained as a deacon seemed to me to be disrespectful to the order of deacons and a challenge to the integrity of my own vocation.

I was left with many questions to ponder, and now that I am Provincial Director of Ordinands, the same questions face me as I oversee the discernment of vocations to diaconate and priesthood in the Scottish Episcopal Church. Why do we discern vocations to the *priesthood* and then ordain candidates as *deacons*—if only for a year? What does ordination to a clerical order mean for a Christian disciple?

Laos and orders

The position I want to explore is that while some people are called by God through the Church to be ordained to a particular role, they do not cease to be members of the whole people of God, the *laos*. As such, they continue to live out their fundamental baptismal calling to the priestly reconciliation, consecration and blessing of the world, and also to the diaconal heralding of God's kingdom within it. That is, whether they are deacons or priests, they remain disciples alongside all of the people of God, called to both loving service and royal priesthood. Priests may look "diaconal" at times, but this belongs to their calling to Christian *diakonia*, not their orders. Similarly, deacons may look "priestly" at times, but this is because they are baptized and share in the royal priesthood of Christ. Priests and deacons are ordained to a particular order to embody and represent one aspect of the baptismal calling of the whole people of God.[4] Let me unpack all this further, with regard firstly to discernment and then to ordination.

Discernment of vocation

Since Vatican II and *Baptism, Eucharist and Ministry*, the Church has found new life in the doctrine of the baptismal calling of Christians. In the baptism rite of the SEC,[5] it is made clear that baptism is the response to God's call—a primary vocation. The promises made describe a priestly and a diaconal vocation:

> to continue in the Apostles' teaching and fellowship, in the breaking of bread and the prayers (priestly) and to proclaim the good news by word and deed, serving Christ in all people, and to work for justice and peace, honouring God in all creation (diaconal).

As baptized disciples we are all called by God to serve in this priestly and diaconal way. But the Spirit also calls some people to inhabit one or other calling in a way that focuses and encourages the baptismal calling of all. Candidates for ordination respond to this call and open themselves to its testing in a process of discernment. The Criteria for Selection that we use are a means of discerning whether God has given someone the charismata that the Church needs to bring about the kingdom on earth. We take considerable time and trouble to define what the criteria are, and then to explore whether there is evidence that a candidate fulfils them. Some of the criteria are shared by deacons and priests—such as qualities of spirituality and faith. Others are different—such as the type of leadership to be exercised and the focus of missional engagement.[6]

This reflects our ecclesiology where we use images of the body and of the Trinity, holding in creative tension oneness and difference; unity and diversity; a common being in Christ and specific gifts and roles which each contribute to the health and holiness of the Body.[7] In the pre-Nicene Church the different orders were understood each to relate to the whole people of God, not to one another. The gift was discerned and the appropriate order assigned.[8]

When we journey with candidates in discernment, the goal is to discover the person within, that unique *character* which is being brought into being by God and developed in relationship, and has the potential to receive *charismata*, gifts of the Spirit for the purpose of building up the body of Christ. Discernment is not only a holy task of serving the Church's needs, but also a pastoral one, of enabling a candidate to live by the reality of their own God-given nature. The deepest question we ask is "Who are you, in God?" If we reach a point where a candidate can respond humbly and securely: "I am called to be a deacon" or "I am called to be a priest", then we have found people who know who they are and who are free to rejoice in others and their gifts. We know that the Church will be enriched by them, and that they will not be impoverished by being asked to give what they do not have.

Thus, when we have spent time and trouble discerning a vocation according to criteria *either* for priesthood *or* diaconate, from first explorations to final assessment and episcopal acceptance, why do we ordain candidates for priesthood to a different vocation, i.e. the diaconate, even if only for a year? What does such a practice say about the integrity of our discernment process and also the integrity of our rites of ordination?

Ordination

I described our baptismal rite above as a public response to God's call to serve the world in a diaconal and priestly way. Our ordination rites are similarly a public response to God's call as heard through the Church. In the Scottish Episcopal Church's Ordinal, we hear the response to God's call in three stages:[9]

1. The *declaration of the candidate* that they are 'truly called' to the Order to which they are to be admitted;

2.   the *assent of the people* who have discerned that the candidate is
     the one whom God has chosen to live and serve in relationship
     with them; and
3.   the *confirmation of the call by the Bishop*, representing the Church
     Universal.

God is the principal agent in ordination, and the Church responds to
God's choice. It is thus a weighty matter to be ordained and for the body
of Christ to call down upon the candidate the sacramental grace that will
enliven and bring to fulfilment the particular gifts and charisms they have
been blessed with for the life of the Church.

To stand before the people of God and the bishop, having spent
months and even years carefully discerning your call to the *priesthood*
and respond to the question, "Do you trust that you are truly called
by God to serve as a *deacon* in the Church" with the words "I do" is a
huge challenge to vocational integrity and, I would argue, to sacramental
integrity, when we ordain "transitional deacons". When I was ordained as
deacon, I could only answer "I do" as an act of obedience to the Church
as represented in my bishop and in recognition that much remains a
mystery to me in my faith and understanding.

Moreover, as many have pointed out, ordaining priests to the
transitional diaconate is a challenge to the vocational integrity of deacons
and their ordination. To spend months and even years carefully discerning
a call to be a deacon, a herald of the kingdom and a commissioned agent
of the Church's mission, and then to watch ordination to the diaconate
being used as a stepping-stone rite for those without that vocation,
diminishes a role that God has created.

Yes, but . . .

There are questions to be answered about this thesis, that we are ordained
to a specific role while continuing our call as baptized disciples to be
diaconal and priestly, whether or not we are ordained to an order in the
Church.

1. Surely priests do what deacons do too?

Yes, because we all do things that others could and probably should do. The day-to-day work of ministry is not always the same as the identified functions of a particular charism of order. A priest might find herself setting up a food bank, but this is because she has not yet motivated the people of God she serves to do that themselves—i.e. a priest's role is to lead a congregation in mission, not to carry out the practical tasks herself. Of course, in her time off, she might well live out her baptismal calling to loving service by helping at a food bank as a Christian disciple, especially if she could rejoice that it had been set up by her colleague the deacon.

But what about the daily pastoral work of a priest? Doesn't visiting and loving care belong to the charism of the priest? Yes, certainly, but the priest is called to pastoral care of the people whom God has entrusted to them in a Christian fellowship. In an established Church, this might well look like everyone in the community, because of the parish system.[10] But essentially the priest gathers and nurtures a congregation and releases its baptismal gifts to serve the world. Such pastoral work that they do often involves a sacramental ministry that belongs to priesthood. Of course, there is going to be dynamic response to need on the part of the priest, who I hope would never refuse care and advocacy to those in need. But we should be clear about the essence of a call, if there is not to be role-creep and a disempowering of those called to exercise other gifts—especially diaconal ones.

2. What about priestly formation? Surely they need a probationary year?

When the bishop ordains someone, he or she recognises in the name of the Church that this person has the potential character and gifts to represent a particular dimension of the Church's discipleship and service. The candidate is no longer in a probationary period; they have been discerned, trained, formed and appraised. If at the end of the normal period of formation, it is judged that the candidate is not yet ready for ordination to the diaconate or priesthood, they should take another year or however long it needs for them to arrive at the point when they can respond, "Yes, I am truly called."

However, it is hard to see how being ordained deacon for a year might help to prove that the candidate will make a good *priest*. Before the advent of seminaries and theological colleges in the nineteenth century, there was a better case for a sustained probationary period, even as a deacon—traditionally priests served as deacons for at least five years.[11] But modern formational programmes take care to equip ordinands for the particular role they will undertake, and having at least some separate formation sessions for priests and deacons is seen as desirable.

At the point of ordination, the candidate's discipleship—their commitment to sharing the new life of Christ in fellowship and mission—should have been tested and proved during formation. Their aptitude for the specific ministry to which they are to be ordained should have been similarly tested and proved. They should be ready to engage in that ministry. That a probationary period as deacon is inappropriate for priests may be seen from ecumenical experience. As J. St H. Gibaut has pointed out, it makes no sense for an experienced minister of word and sacrament who is transferring to the Anglican Church to be required to be ordained deacon before ordination as priest, and indeed sometimes this diaconal ordination has been dispensed with.[12]

Thus, as disciples and as ordinands, candidates should be directly ordained to either the diaconate or the priesthood as and when the Church is satisfied that they can respond to its call with integrity and competence.

3. Doesn't saying that you are a priest in this bit of your life and a disciple in that bit divide up your vocational identity in an unhelpful way?

I have certainly found that living as a priest has integrated much of my life, and I imagine that deacons would say the same. But the root of my identity in Christ is my baptism and the promises I owned for myself at my confirmation. Each one of us will live out our Christian discipleship in a different way—some of my life is clearly serving as a priest in a congregation, some is as a wife and mother, some is as an unofficial chaplain to a secular singing group I go to, some is as a campaigner for farmers in Malawi.

In all these activities I am still the same person who comes before God in prayer and commitment. But I have clarity about the order of ministry to which I have been called and how I should relate to the whole people of God. In fact, it has been pointed out that retaining two orders within the same person is more confusing than seeing oneself as a disciple who is also a deacon or a priest. For example, if a priest (who has been ordained a transitional deacon) is vested as a "liturgical deacon" before a service, and someone asks for confession and absolution, what should be their response?[13]

So my perspective on the transitional diaconate from the point of view of a priest is that it undermines the integrity of our discernment processes and of ordination. We are called to respond as disciples to God's call in baptism, to the service, reconciliation and consecration of the world; some are also called to respond as ministers to God's call in ordination, holding up to the Church the diaconal or priestly facets of our common call as Christians. In the words of the command in 1 Peter 4:10:

> Like good stewards of the manifold grace of God, serve one another with whatever gift each of you has received.

Notes

1   *Truly Called by God to Serve as a Deacon. The Report of the Bishops' Working Group on the Distinctive Diaconate* (available from General Synod Office of the SEC: Edinburgh, 1987).

2   *Baptism, Eucharist and Ministry*, Faith and Order Paper no. 111 (World Council of Churches, Geneva, 1982).

3   Notably Steven Croft, *Ministry in Three Dimensions: Ordination and Leadership in the Local Church* (London: DLT, 2008).

4   Cf. *The Iona Report: Final Report of the Task Force on the Diaconate*, Anglican Church of Canada, Faith, Worship and Ministry, Appendix 3 (2016), pp. 11–12.

5   Holy Baptism 2006 (General Synod Office, Edinburgh 2006), see <https://www.scotland.anglican.org/who-we-are/publications/liturgies>.

[6]   Details of the discernment process in the SEC can be found at <https://www.
scotland.anglican.org/who-we-are/vocation-and-ministry>.

[7]   R. David Cox, *Priesthood in a New Millennium* (New York: Church Publishing,
2004), p. 317, suggests that metaphors of the Body and of the Trinity might
indicate the possibility of direct ordination, but argues that they also allow a
person to have different roles, such as deacon and priest, at the same time.

[8]   L. Weil, "Aspects of the issue of *Per Saltum* ordination: an Anglican
Perspective", in Nathan Mitchell and John F. Baldwin (eds), *Rule of Prayer,
Rule of Faith: Essays in Honor of Aidan Kavanagh OSB* (Collegeville: Liturgical
Press, 1996), pp. 200–217, here p. 203.

[9]   Scottish Ordinal 1984 (amended 2006) (General Synod Office: Edinburgh,
2006), see <https://www.scotland.anglican.org/who-we-are/publications/
liturgies>.

[10]   Thus R. David Cox (above, n. 7), p. 318, argues that the diaconate is inherent
in the Anglican concept of parochial priesthood, as self-sacrificing service to
"the flock"; but such service is not consonant with modern understandings
of the diaconate as a herald of the gospel to the wider community.

[11]   J. St H. Gibaut, "Considering the Possibility of Direct Ordination" in
Equipping the Saints: Ordination in Anglicanism Today. Papers from the 6th
International Anglican Liturgical Consultation (Dublin: Columba Press,
2006), pp. 85–104, here pp. 86–90.

[12]   Gibaut (above, n.11), pp. 93–100.

[13]   An example given by L. Weil (above, n. 8), pp. 213–214.

PART 3

Women and the Diaconate

CHAPTER 5

Women and the Diaconate: An Artistic and Historical Perspective

Maylanne Maybee, with Terrie Chedore

This chapter is accompanied by images featured in the artistic work of Terrie Chedore, a diaconal artist, as part of a study, "Colouring Outside the Lines: Exploring parallels in the histories of diaconal ministry and religious art". She created seven distinct icons or images of the most significant historical periods in the evolution of diakonia through using seashells and bits of beach debris. In Zen-like fashion, the final creations were dismantled and the found items returned to the ocean. All that remains are the digital photographs. The images in this presentation are copyrighted by Terrie Chedore (www. tjchedore.ca), and the artist retains reproduction rights in perpetuity.

The role of women in the diaconate needs to be considered in the context of the history and evolution of the diaconate since its origins in scripture and the early Church, bearing in mind that there is no single model and no precise and unchanging definition of the diaconate to hold on to. Nevertheless, we can find a consistent thread if we go beyond a particular focus on the offices or orders of deacons, deaconesses or diaconal ministers and look instead for common characteristics of diaconal ministry.

In Jesus' own ministry, he carried out his sacred mission, his *diakonia*, by the way he cared for the poor and healed the sick, by his style of teaching in parables, by his prophetic challenging of people of wealth and religious privilege. In the fourth Gospel, John's story of Jesus washing the feet of the disciples (John 13:1–10) sums up his life as a *diakonos*, setting

Image 1—Jesus: Rabbi, teacher, companion, friend

I am among you as [ὁ διακονῶν] the One who serves.
(Luke 22:27)

This first image of Terrie Chedore shows Jesus "cloaked in
mystery", partially hidden by the mists of history, by differing
accounts in Scripture and by centuries of interpretation.

an example for others to do the same: "If I, your Lord and Teacher, have washed your feet, you also ought to wash one another's feet".

Scriptural references to deacons do not tell us specifically what deacons are or do. It was assumed that the reader would know. Chapter 6 in the Book of Acts is often cited as an account of the first deacons, though the word for "deacon" is not applied to them. The Jesus community in Jerusalem was experiencing tensions arising from cultural differences and the allocation of resources in a period of rapid growth. They selected seven men for the laying on of hands to extend and diversify the ministry of the apostles and to ensure the fair distribution of food and the Word among the Greek widows. Thus, a characteristic of *diakonia* was its flexibility of function within the Church's authorized ministry.

1 Timothy, dated about 100 CE, gives a more nuanced description of the diaconate as an office. "Deacons must be men of grave behaviour; they must be examined and if found blameless may afterwards serve as deacons. The women must be of grave behaviour . . . " Though there are different ways of interpreting this passage, one is to understand it as referring to women deacons. In fact, Origen of Alexandria (c. 185–254) comments on this text when writing about the value of the women's diaconate.[1] Other evidence that favours the likelihood of women in the diaconate is found in Romans 16:10, which refers to Phoebe of Cenchraea as *diakonos*, the same word used for male deacons. Subsequent liturgies of the early Church used ordination prayers for women that referred to "the order of Phoebe, whom the apostle [Paul] ordained as minister (deacon) in Cenchraea".[2]

Terrie Chedore comments that from the first to the third centuries, roles and functions in ministry were shared among women and men alike, and both were ordained to diaconal positions in rites that were very similar. While some scholars have discounted the status of women within the order, saying their role was merely functional, others convincingly argue that the ordination of women deacons would have had the same sacramental significance as that for male deacons.

Image 2—Phoebe, the Deacon

*I commend to you our sister, Phoebe, a deacon
of the church in Cenchraea.*
(Romans 16:1)

Diakonia: Humble service? Commissioned task?

The Australian scholar John Collins conducted a study in the 1990s comparing the use of *diakon-* words in Christian scripture to their use in contemporary Greek literature.[3] The results of his analysis are causing us to rethink our assumptions: is *diakonia* about servants who engage in humble service or about agents or go-betweens who carry out a commissioned task? Whatever its core meaning, the pattern of ministry that we can observe after the first century is a movement away from an itinerant, charismatic style of leadership described in Acts and the epistles to one that is more fixed. (The Dutch scholar and church historian Edward Schillebeeckx notes that a community without a good, matter-of-fact pastoral institutionalization of its ministry ran the risk of losing the apostolicity and thus the Christian character of its origin.[4])

Thus, toward the second century, we witness a more settled and standardized leadership. The threefold model of bishop, presbyter and deacon began to develop and solidify. The functions of deacons varied region to region. Their duties could include:

- Distributing the sacraments to families who were absent from the assembly
- Administering baptism
- Acting as doorkeepers, with one door for men and one door for women
- Giving instructions to the assembly
- Making announcements
- Keeping order in church; keeping people awake
- Watching behaviour (this was important in times of persecution)
- Reciting the bidding prayer, which assumed knowledge of the needs of the community
- Reading the Gospel or epistle
- In some places preaching; in others not
- Fanning the chalice to keep flies away from the wine
- Dismissing the congregation.

Image 3 – Jesus the Christ – sixth century

For the Lord our God the Almighty reigns.
(Revelation 19:6b)

This sixth-century image of Jesus the Christ, based on a Byzantine Trinitarian icon of *The Christ Pantocrator*, is in stark contrast with the first of Chedore's images showing a figure cloaked in mystery.

"The fleshed-out Christology depicted here – *not human, nor God, nor Spirit, but all of these things together* – was not part of the first- and second-century understanding of Jesus. By the sixth century, the Bible was a closed canon compiled into one book, and the cross had become the official symbol of Christianity."

The functions of women in the diaconate during this period were similar to those of men, usually carried out with and among other women. They would give instruction to women in their home, assist at the baptism of women, act as doorkeepers in church and conduct women to their seats, and visit women who were sick and afflicted.

After the conversion of the emperor Constantine and the full recognition of Christianity in 325, everything began to change. It brought an end to the persecution of Christians and an increase in the number of adult baptisms. In Byzantine practice, baptism and the anointing of the sick became increasingly elaborate rites, requiring the presence of ordained deacons and the help of dedicated women. Some historians consider that such women were very likely ordained for these tasks and date the ordination of women to the full diaconate to this period.[5] At the same time, the Church's ascendance to political and social prominence brought about a significant change in the culture of flexibility and urgency that characterized the early centuries of Christian ministry.

In Western Christendom, the Council of Nicaea imposed new restrictions on deacons: they were no longer authorized to preside at the Eucharist and were placed below bishops and presbyters in status. The diaconate gained functions and authority in the liturgy, but began to be reduced to a transitional stage of ordination to the priesthood. A statement of the Council regarding the status of women in the diaconate has been interpreted as meaning that women were never really ordained, though its meaning is ambiguous and probably refers to the situation in a particular community rather than deaconesses across the board.

Regardless, the order of deaconess, especially in the West, fell into abeyance after Nicaea and by the sixth century had all but disappeared. Chedore describes this shift in the period between the fourth and sixth centuries as going from equality to imbalance.

The Middle Ages

The Middle Ages (approximately 400 to 1500 of the Common Era) saw the ascendance of monastic orders, originating with those desert fathers and mothers who lived lives of extreme self-denial. Eventually, under the

Image 4—From equality to imbalance: Deacons in the developing Church

There is no longer slave or free, there is no longer male or female; for all of you are one in Christ.
(Galatians 3:28)

While the two figures shown in her icon appear to be engaged in conversation, they are actually moving in different directions, moving past each other.

leadership of figures like Benedict of Nursia, monastics became more communal. While many led a life of prayer and agricultural work, some orders took on the role of service to those in need. Although the order of deaconesses disappeared in both East and West in the course of the Middle Ages, the ministry of women did not. When Francis (himself a deacon) started his order, the Poor Clares were formed alongside them. In Belgium and other parts of Europe, the Béguines, a lay order of women, emerged and flourished, along with other women's communities dedicated to working with the poor.

This was also an age when creativity and independent thinking were deeply suspected. Artists, women and free thinkers were feared and persecuted. Some were burnt at the stake. Of this period, Chedore writes:

> Accusations of idolatry and heresy, along with experiences of iconoclasm and inquisition, remained constant threats throughout the Middle Ages and into the Protestant Reformation. Two significant periods of iconoclasm (during the eighth and ninth centuries and again during the fifteenth and sixteenth centuries) severely impacted the creativity of artists and the diaconate.

These episodes of persecution and iconoclasm seem to represent the ongoing struggle between control and creativity, between those concerned with protecting the tradition, orthodoxy and stability of the institutional Church and those inspired by the diaconal spirit of creativity and compassion, concerned with caring for strangers and outcasts and giving free expression to their own God-given gifts. Nevertheless, the forces of adaptation and goodwill prevailed among communities of women and men who sought to respond with mercy and justice to those at the margins of church and society.

Image 5—Idolatry, heresy, iconoclasm and inquisition

If one member suffers, all suffer.
(1 Corinthians 12:26)

Chedore used seaweed and other detritus
from the beach to create this image.

The Reformation and after

During the Reformation, Martin Luther developed a theology of "the priesthood of all believers", removing a strict hierarchical pattern between higher and lower orders of Christians. Though he did not say much about the diaconate, he expressed a preference for deacons who provided service to the poor rather than focusing on their liturgical roles. Different reformers created a diaconate to fit their theology and needs. Calvin proposed four offices for clergy as pastors, elders, doctors and deacons. Deacons tended to be well-to-do gentlemen, charged with handling money and caring for the poor. The only role in ministry open to women was being a pastor's wife.

The Counter-Reformation was the term given to the response of the Catholic Church to the Reformation, as deliberated at the Council of Trent from 1545 to 1563. The Church revisited the role of deacons, reducing them to a lower order and limiting their liturgical role to reading the Gospel and distributing the bread. They served the bishop, letting him know what was going on, and could explain the Gospel—but not from the pulpit. In Anglicanism, the threefold order of ministry was retained. The diaconate, inherited from pre-Reformation Catholicism, was now a mere formality on the way to priesthood. The 1550 Ordinal refers to the diaconate as "this inferior office". Prior to that date, the Roman Pontifical remained in use for ordinations in Henry VIII's Church of England, and the rite for making deacons remained relatively unaltered in the 1662 *Book of Common Prayer*.

In modern times the order of deaconesses underwent a resurgence. Responding to the changing social conditions in the Industrial Revolution and the growing need for humanitarian service, Pastor Theodor Fliedner founded a women's training school in Kaiserswerth, Germany. It offered rigorous training for women in nursing, teaching and social work, as well as formation in a deep inner spiritual life. (Its most famous student, Florence Nightingale, never became a deaconess herself.) The movement spread from Germany to England, where in 1863 Elizabeth Ferard received a deaconess's licence, making her the first deaconess in the Church of England and in the Anglican Communion. She founded a community for women religious serving in the diaconal tradition in

Image 6—The spirit of *diakonia*

To do justice, and to love kindness, and to walk humbly with your God.
(Micah 6:8)

Chedore's sixth image shows the continuity of the *diakonia*
of women as well as men "outside the authority of the
church", leading toward the emergence of a renewed
diaconate during the Protestant Reformation.

London's King's Cross and later in Notting Hill. Twenty years later, like many other women who broke new ground, her "health failed", and she died in 1883.

Deaconesses in the Anglican Communion

The Church of England Deaconess Missionary and Training House, the first training school for women of this kind in Canada, was founded in Toronto in 1892. The Methodists and Presbyterians soon followed. The Social Gospel movement, combined with the influence of early feminism, and the overseas missionary movement gave momentum to these schools. The Centre for Christian Studies, established in 1969, represents the bringing together of these traditions. It is now an ecumenical (Anglican–United) theological school in Winnipeg. What we see here is the coalescing of the notion of *diakonia* as a commissioned task or sacred mission, carried out in the spirit of Jesus' care for the poor and the sick, by women who were excluded from other orders of ministry. The seventh icon developed by Terrie Chedore celebrates the hope of this movement.

Elizabeth Ferard had written in her work, *Of the Deaconess Office in General*, dated 1861:[6]

> Deaconesses have, according to the apostolical regulations, the office of serving the Christian congregation as Phoebe served the Church at Cenchraea. To them is committed the care of the sick, the poor, the education of your children, and generally the help of the needy of whatever kind. And also it is their office to be helpers, either directly or indirectly, of the ministers of the Church.
>
> They must, therefore, have the qualities which the Apostle requires from deacons (Acts 6:8). They must first, be of good report; and second, be full of faith and good works.

In these two paragraphs Ferard connects women and *diakonia* with the early Church and describes them as equal in status and function to the

Image 7—Hope on the horizon

I found a new heaven and a new earth.
(Revelation 21:1)

seven men set aside by the apostles in Acts 6. She did not live to witness the recognition of the order of deaconesses by the Lambeth Conference of 1897, in a resolution stating "That this Conference recognizes with thankfulness the revival alike of brotherhoods and sisterhoods and of the office of deaconesses in our branch of the Church . . . ".

The Lambeth Conference of 1920 carried things further in acknowledging that "The time has come when, in the interests of the Church at large . . . the diaconate of women should be restored formally and canonically, and should be recognized throughout the Anglican Communion" (Resolution 47 of the 1920 Lambeth Conference). There was, however, a significant caveat: "The office of deaconess is primarily a ministry of succour, bodily and spiritual, especially to women, and should follow the lines of the primitive rather than of the modern diaconate of men" (Resolution 49).

The Lambeth Conference of 1968 recognized that the diaconate integrated service of others with liturgical functions and recommended that it include both women and men and that the Ordinal be revised to reflect a new role for the diaconate and remove any reference to it as "an inferior office". It further recommended that deaconesses who had received the laying-on of hands with prayer should be considered to be within the diaconate.

Conclusion

Regarding women in the priesthood, after some fifty years of discussion, the 1968 Lambeth Conference also recognized that at present "the arguments for and against the ordination of women to the priesthood are inconclusive" and that dissent on this issue would continue.

Seventeen years later, in 1985, the position of the Anglican Communion was summarized in a letter from the Archbishop of Canterbury, Robert Runcie, to Cardinal Willebrands under these key points:

- Holy Scripture and tradition present no fundamental objection to the ordination of women;

- By itself, the witness of the New Testament does not permit a clear settlement of the question;
- Tradition appears to be open to this development;
- The exclusion of women from the priestly ministry cannot be proved to be by "divine law".[7]

Furthermore, Runcie gave compelling reasons from an Anglican perspective of why women should be ordained. The first was Christological—that Christ's humanity is inclusive of women—and the second was ecclesiological—that women's participation in the ministerial priesthood "more perfectly" represents Christ's inclusive high priesthood.

Today, though there is not yet consensus in the Anglican Communion on the role of women in the priesthood or the episcopate, the face of our Church and its leadership has changed irrevocably. As one scholar stated, "Notions of equality, equity and justice have not necessarily prevailed over the authority of church tradition, but have profoundly affected it."[8]

Women bishops in the Anglican Communion attending the 2008 Lambeth Conference. (Photo: Marites N. Sison, 2008. © The Anglican Journal, General Synod, The Anglican Church of Canada.)

Notes

1   Origen of Alexandria. See John Wijngaards, *No Women in Holy Orders? The Women Deacons of the Early Church* (Norwich: Canterbury Press, 2002), p. 15.

2   From an ordination prayer derived from the Liturgy of St James used in the early Christian Church in Jerusalem. F. C. Conybeare and O. Wardrop, "The Georgian Version of the Liturgy of St James", *Revue de l'Orient chrétien* 19 (1914), pp. 23–53. Quoted in the above, p. 86.

3   John N. Collins, *Diakonia: Re-interpreting the Ancient Sources* (Oxford University Press, originally published in 1990).

4   Edward Schillebeeckx, *Ministry: Leadership in the Community of Jesus Christ* (New York: Crossroad, 1981), p. 24.

5   J. G. Davies, "Deacons, Deaconesses and Minor Orders in the Patristic Period", *Journal of Ecclesiastical History* 14 (1963), pp. 1–23.

6   See Robert Atwell, *Celebrating the Saints* (Norwich: Canterbury Press, 2016), p. 265.

7   Letter of Robert Runcie, Archbishop of Canterbury, to Cardinal Jan Willebrands, President of the Vatican Secretariat for Promoting Christian Unity, 18 December 1985.

8   Noel Cox, *The Catholicity of Ordained Ministry in the Anglican Communion: An Examination of the Ecclesiology Implicit in the Validity of Orders Debate* (Saarbrücken: VDM Verlag Dr. Müller, 2009), p. 88.

CHAPTER 6

Women and the Diaconate: A Roman Catholic Perspective

Gloria Marie Jones, OP

I explore the question of women and the diaconate, conscious that my contribution, my perspective, is clearly shaped by my identity as a Dominican Sister, by experience as a woman and sister in the community of the Roman Catholic Church in California, and as a citizen of the United States . . . challenging and often embarrassing reality at this moment!

I believe the heart of this question is so much more significant than simply giving women more power, or status as some might see it. I believe at the heart of this question is not just past history. Our reflection on this question needs to be grounded fundamentally in our responsibility, our call as church, to be faithful to Jesus' mission that he passed on to ALL of us, baptized in Christ—to live in his Spirit, to be bearers of his grace in our world today.

I believe this question of women deacons is best addressed in light of the mission of the Church and the context facing us in the Church and the wider social order today. The Church exists at the service of Jesus' mission. The Second Vatican Council recognized that the Church needed a new form of ordained ministry that modelled Christ the Servant. Deacons are the symbol of the call we all share as baptized Christians—to be people of God's Word, sent forth to respond to the spiritual and corporal needs of God's people. Deacons are called to animate and sacramentalize the Church's call to service. They are the sign and symbol of what is the heart of the whole Church. As a member of the Roman Catholic Church, I struggle with the question: how are the power and reality of that sign and symbol impacted by the fact that only half of the Church, those who are male, are able to *be* this symbol? Why should that be? What does that mean to all of the female members of our Church?

I bring to this question my own history as the daughter of a deacon, who personally witnessed my mother's faithful and wholehearted participation in my father's extensive and intensive preparation for ordination. It was clearly a shared commitment. At my father's ordination, a most moving event for me, I was conscious of my mother, sitting in the pew with us, her daughters, as we witnessed his ordination. And I know of her faithful companioning of him, her presence, support and engagement, as he ministered the sacrament of baptism, agonized over his preaching preparation, and walked with those mourning the loss of loved ones through his bereavement ministry. It was truly a shared preparation and ministry . . . but one was ordained and the other was not. In my reflection on all of this, the thought has occurred to me: through the Sacrament of Matrimony, they became one body. How good and right it would be, how powerful, if their sacramental union could be further expressed, rather than diminished, through this sacrament of ordination to the diaconate—not as a requirement for everyone, certainly, but as an option for married couples.

We know that through the years women of all walks of life have been ministers of *diakonia* in the Church. In fact, we know women have significantly impacted the Roman Church in the areas of catechetical ministry, liturgical ministry, pastoral ministry, ministry to the sick, all ministries appropriate to the diaconate role. I have listened to my Dominican Sisters' heartfelt frustration as chaplains in hospitals, where they experience over and over again the critical need and desire of patients for reconciliation and anointing. When priests are not available they have no ability to respond, to offer the power of Jesus' presence through sacramental grace at these moments of such significant vulnerability and need. Could this be the will of Jesus for his people?

I join Cardinal Döpfner of the Archdiocese of Munich-Freising in his question: why deny those who are serving in diaconal roles the grace of this sacrament?[1] Would this not strengthen our Church? Would it not strengthen and support those engaged in this ministry? Vatican II's teaching about the diaconate was grounded in the Church's understanding of grace as God's gift to the entire people of God, both men and women. What is lost when we try to portion out or limit sacramental grace? Why would we do such a thing? Is this what Jesus taught his disciples as he sent them forth to heal and teach and be instruments of God's kingdom of mercy and healing and love?

I claim no expertise regarding the ordination of women to the diaconate. But I give thanks for recent experiences that have drawn me to this question and stretched my own understanding as well as increased my questions. Over the past few years, I have had the honour to engage in several dialogues on the question of women deacons:

- the first, in 2015, when I joined Gary Macy at Stanford University;
- the second, in April 2017 with Bishop Randolph Calvo, canonist who was head of the American Canonical Society in 1995, when it concluded its study related to women deacons;
- and lastly, in January 2018, when I facilitated a seminar day in which Deacon William Ditewig was a major presenter.

Most especially, I give thanks for the opportunity to participate in the meeting of the International Union of Superiors General (UISG) in Rome, in May 2016, which became the catalyst for Pope Francis to establish the commission to study the possibility of women deacons in the Roman Catholic Church. I want to share about this experience, a story not sufficiently known. I think it speaks to this question of women's role in the Church.

Every three years, the International Union of Superiors General invites women religious congregational leaders to gather in Rome for a week's assembly. Some eight to nine hundred congregational leaders from eighty different countries on every continent gather. Interpretation is provided in ten plus languages! It is truly an experience of the universal Church and provides the opportunity for women religious leaders to address critical issues facing consecrated religious life. In the context of this gathering we traditionally have an audience with the Pope at the Vatican.

In 2013, we gathered with Pope Francis just a month after his election. The gathering was both formal and brief. Pope Francis addressed us in Italian and unfortunately interpretation equipment was not available.

The impact of the exchange was disappointing. Three years later, on 12 May 2016, the eight hundred and fifty-four members of our assembly found our way to the Paul VI Audience Hall at the Vatican. This time we all had interpretation equipment. Most significant to this encounter was the fact that prior to the gathering Pope Francis invited the UISG to submit questions we would like him to address in our gathering. This was definitely a first! In the months prior to our assembly, the UISG Coordinating Council gathered questions from the various continents. They studied the recommendations and formulated the final six questions which were presented to Pope Francis prior to the meeting.

Interestingly, even though Pope Francis had received the questions prior to the meeting, he requested that each question be presented orally to him by a sister. That was significant. It is one thing to submit questions in writing, but another thing to present the questions personally and publicly to Pope Francis, especially those that were considered controversial by some. In truth, the questions and the exchange were both honest and challenging regarding women's role in the Church, obstacles consecrated women religious face in our lives and ministry, the obstacle canon law can present in dealing with present reality in religious life, the need for women's voices to be heard. Pope Francis addressed each with his characteristic open, honest, personal, non-defensive style, often affirming our life experience and frustrations through the sharing of his own personal frustration he experienced as a bishop. The quality of his person, his spirit, was experienced through his heartfelt response.

The first question set the larger context for the question about the diaconate . . . in order to give a fuller flavour of the exchange:

> Pope Francis, you said that "the feminine genius is needed in all expressions in the life of society . . . and in the Church", and yet women are excluded from decision-making processes in the Church, especially at the highest levels, and from preaching at the Eucharist. An important obstacle to the Church's full embrace of "feminine genius" is the bond that decision-making processes and preaching both have with priestly ordination. Do you see a way of separating leadership roles and preaching at the Eucharist from

ordination, so that our Church can be more open to receiving the genius of women in the very near future?

A good question, is it not? You will have to read his response online: <https://w2.vatican.va/content/francesco/en/speeches/2016/may/ documents/papa-francesco_20160512_uisg.html>.

Building on that, the second question addressed the role of consecrated women in the Church and raised the question of the ordination of women to the diaconate. I want to share with you both the entire question and Pope Francis' response.

> Pope Francis, consecrated women already do much work with the poor and the marginalized, they teach catechism, they accompany the sick and the dying, they distribute Communion; in many countries they lead the communal prayers in the absence of a priest and in those circumstances they give a homily. In the Church there is the office of the permanent diaconate, but it is open only to men, married or not. What prevents the Church from including women among permanent deacons, as was the case in the primitive Church? Why not constitute an official commission to study the matter? Can you give us an example of where you see the possibility of better integration of women and consecrated women in the life of the Church?

Pope Francis responded:

> This question goes in the direction of "doing": consecrated women already do much work with the poor, they do many things . . . And it touches on the problem of the permanent diaconate. . . . Indeed this existed in early times: there was a beginning . . . I remember that it was a theme which interested me considerably when I came to Rome for meetings, and I stayed at the Domus Paolo VI; there was a good Syrian theologian there, who had produced a critical edition and translation of the Hymns of Ephrem the Syrian. One day I asked him about this, and he explained to me that in the early times of the Church there were

some deaconesses. But what were these deaconesses? Were they ordained or not? The Council of Chalcedon (in 451) speaks about this, but it is somewhat unclear. What was the role of deaconesses in those times? It seems—I was told by this man, who is now dead but who was a good professor, wise and erudite—it seems that the role of the deaconesses was to help in the baptism of women, with their immersion; for the sake of decorum they baptized them; and also anointed the body of women, in baptism. And another curious fact: when there was a judgement on a marriage because a husband beat his wife and she went to the bishop to lay a complaint, deaconesses were responsible for inspecting the bruises left on the woman's body from her husband's blows, and for informing the bishop. This I remember.

There are various publications on the diaconate in the Church, but it is not clear how it was in the past. I think I will ask the Congregation for the Doctrine of the Faith to refer me to some studies on this theme, because I have answered you only on the basis of what I heard from this priest, who was a learned and good researcher, on the permanent diaconate. In addition, I would like to constitute an official commission to study the question: I think it will be good for the Church to clarify this point; I agree, and I will speak [to the Congregation] in order to do something of this nature.

And thus the formation of the commission was set into being. It is with a sense of humble pride that I share this story with you. Religious women spoke the truth of our experience. We did this not simply for ourselves but on behalf of all women. We did it on behalf of the Church and of all God's people. I believe the heart of our UISG inquiry was about much more than simply ordination of women to the diaconate, although that would be a significant step forward. The heart of our inquiry is how the present structure of the Church might be more open and more flexible to allow the gift of feminine genius, as Pope Francis called it, to be at the service of the Church and all of God's people in a fuller, sacramental context. I believe the answer regarding the ordination of women to the diaconate is much more than simply a historical one. We are not meant simply to replicate the experience of the early Church. The early Church, under the inspiration of the Spirit, responded to the needs of the moment and how the followers of The Way would continue Jesus' own ministry/presence marked by mercy, inclusivity, and the experience of God's reign of Love.

We share the same mandate. How is our Church today called to give credible witness to Jesus, to his saving presence? How do we as church continue the preaching of the kingdom as fully and effectively as possible? This is the only mission worthy of the Church today. I have come to believe that the ordination of women to the diaconate is important for the sake of the Church, much more than for the sake of women. My conviction is strengthened by Cardinal Suenens' words during the Vatican Council:

> The Church is entitled to all of the grace the Holy Spirit provides.
> It is important not to close off any means by which the grace of
> God might flow.[2]

This applies to both men and women.

The Canon Law Society of America, in its 1995 study of the question of women deacons, concluded with the statement:

> The ordination of women to the permanent diaconate is possible
> and may even be desirable for the United States in its present
> cultural condition.[3]

What would keep us from acting upon this, if this is true?

Notes

[1]   See Gerald O'Collins, "Unlock the Door", *The Tablet*, 25 May 2013, pp. 4–5.

[2]   AS II/II, 227–230.

[3]   *The Canonical Implications of Ordaining Women to the Permanent Diaconate: Report of an Ad Hoc Committee of the Canon Law Society of America*, Washington DC, 1995, section F, Summary.

CHAPTER 7

Women Deacons in the Christian East: What is the State of the Question?

Brian A. Butcher

Introduction

In this chapter, let us treat, albeit briefly, the phenomenon of women deacons or deaconesses—the alternate names being themselves indicative of the ambiguity attending this office in the Christian East, whether on a level of theory or pastoral practice. There are, and historically have been, discrete traditions: multiple renditions, so to speak, on a common theme. Here it will be possible only to sketch the shape of the ministry in question, focusing particularly on its limited contemporary expressions.

For decades, the Christian East has served as a quarry from which scholars have mined evidence for a predominantly Western debate; increasingly, however, the Eastern Churches are becoming fora in their own right for reflection (and experimentation) in regard to the female diaconate.[1] Two key concerns animate those who approach the revival of the office first and foremost as a matter of Orthodox tradition—rather than, say, on the basis of desiderata related to the perceived needs of the Church in our day, or as a matter of ecumenical rapprochement. These concerns are, firstly, the nature of the historical precedents for women deacons in the Eastern Churches and, secondly, the theological principles informing said precedents. On both counts, the matter is not without controversy, since interest in the past is portentous for the present and future of the Church: for determining what are (or ought to be) the criteria regulating a reinvigorated ministry of women deacons today.

Byzantine/Eastern Orthodox precedents

It has become widely known that the practice of the Church of Constantinople, throughout the first millennium, was to ordain women deacons within the sanctuary in a rite of ordination (*cheirotonia*) very similar to that used for male deacons. We need not rehearse the history here, as it has been meticulously documented.[2] While the female diaconate gradually fell into desuetude in Byzantium, it has enjoyed sporadic instances of revival in modern times, including that of St Nektarios of Pentapolis (1846–1920), who ordained monastic women deacons in 1911 for Holy Trinity Convent in Aegina, as well as that of Metropolitan Christodoulos (then of Demetrias), who similarly ordained a woman deacon in 1986.

Ecumenical Patriarch Bartholomew I propelled matters forward in the 1990s by expressing his principled commitment to restoring the office. For instance, in his "Address to the Inter-Orthodox Conference for Women (Phanar, Istanbul: May 12 1997)", he 1) asserts that the ministry of women deacons is a venerable element of Orthodox tradition; 2) acknowledges an increasing desire among Orthodox faithful to reap the pastoral benefits of such a ministry; and 3) affirms that contemporary women may in fact already be called to diaconal service.[3] In turn, a 2004 synod of the Church of Greece voted to allow bishops the discretion to ordain women deacons in isolated monastic contexts, where no priest was available—although by all accounts this resolution has yet to be actually implemented.

Similarly, in 2016, the Greek Orthodox Patriarchate of Alexandria—not the much larger Coptic Orthodox Church also rooted in that city, but rather its Chalcedonian, Byzantine-Rite counterpart—determined that it would restore the office of deaconess. In 2017, Patriarch Theodore II proceeded to implement this decision to a limited degree by ordaining (*cheirothesia*) a Congolese nun a "deaconess of the mission" and consecrating several others to church service. This event, alternately touted and reprobated on social media, was admittedly idiosyncratic.[4] The Byzantine rite of subdiaconal ordination was not used, but only the prayers used for the orders below it, i.e. those for reader/chanter and for one entering ecclesiastical ministry. Nonetheless, the photographs of the event indicate that the candidates in question were given ewers, pitchers and towels to wash the patriarch's hands, in the manner customary for subdeacons.

Armenian precedents

While there is evidence from the first millennium for the office of deaconess in the Armenian Church, it is principally to the revival of the order from the 1700s onward that recent scholarly attention has been directed.[5] This is so, because the eighteenth-century practice, unlike that of earlier centuries, unequivocally witnesses to a unique phenomenon, namely, that of women deacons enjoying a status and role identical to that of their male peers. Armenian deaconesses are deacons who are women, rather than women constituting a distinct, if in some instances parallel, order—the norm elsewhere in the Christian Orient.[6]

Until very recently, the small corps of Armenian deaconesses included only a handful of elderly nuns in Lebanon, as well as one in Istanbul, Mother Hrip'sime of Constantinople, ordained in 1982. To the surprise of many, however, the Armenian Archbishop of Tehran, Sebouh Sarkissian, decided in 2017 to ordain a twenty-three-year-old laywoman as a "parish deacon"; this was the first ordination of a female diaconal candidate in several decades and apparently the first ever instance of a non-monastic woman being so ordained. A further novelty is the clear indication that Ani-Kristi Manvelian, as a non-monastic deacon, will remain free to pursue marriage in the future—a privilege generally conceded to Armenian deacons (as explained in my other contribution to the present volume). Thus, she may end up being both the first non-monastic woman deacon and the first non-celibate.[7]

Reflections

The burgeoning literature on the female diaconate in the Christian East has raised as many questions as it has answered, not least because the sources are not unanimous concerning the status or rank of women deacons vis-à-vis other ministries. There are not insignificant discrepancies *between* the Eastern Churches in terms of the history of the office in their respective contexts; paradoxically, however, it does not seem to have ever become a *casus belli*, suggesting that its renewal in one or another Church may not portend the kind of division that some might fear. Historical precedents notwithstanding, however, it is clear that even discussions of women deacons (and, *a fortiori*, the initiative of the Patriarchate of Alexandria described above) *are* proving to be quite controversial among Eastern Orthodox churches. And anecdotal evidence suggests that the Archbishop Sarkissian's *sui generis* initiative has not been well received elsewhere in the Armenian Apostolic Church, not least by the Catholicos of All Armenians, Karekin II, based in Etchmiadzin. Only time will tell if Tehran's new cleric will be not only the first such deaconess but also the last.

The question of whether (and how) to revive the ministry of women deacons in the Eastern Churches does not admit of any ready answer, not least because it serves as an index to a number of other, as yet unresolved matters, both theoretical and practical: these include biblical (specifically Old Testament) taboos concerning ritual (im)purity, still widely observed in the Christian East, and the persistence of traditional gender roles in many contexts—although the reality is in fact more complex than one might be inclined to think.[8] Western Christians will likely be perplexed, if not scandalized, by these, not least because they are habituated to current Western cultural norms being accepted and emulated in their respective faith communities. Let us in conclusion turn our attention in this direction.

Undoubtedly, there are hermeneutical challenges attending any significant change in the status quo. While a key premise of those seeking to revive the order is that "what the Church has done the Church can do again", few accept that restoration of the female diaconate in the twenty-first century should be delimited *a priori* by the actual ambit of the ministry as given in the historical record—especially because the paucity of extant evidence provides less than a full picture of the role of women deacons in the past.[9] One thinks here of the oft-quoted maxim of the great Eastern liturgist Robert Taft that "history is instructive, but not normative". History, that is, proves itself a two-edged sword: the uncontestable *fact* of women's ordination to diaconate is counterbalanced by the distinct status and roles which characterized their ministry—not least in the very limited liturgical responsibilities traditionally allotted them.[10]

Moreover, many agree that it is pastorally impractical, even unreasonable, for a deaconess to do less than her counterpart in contemporary lay ministry, whether male or female. And yet Eastern Christians remain generally averse to any suggestion that historical distinctions in ministry roles are ultimately due to merely transient, if not arbitrary, social conventions. For example, the vesture of deaconesses (even in the case of the Armenians) has always been distinctive—as if to accentuate that femininity is not suppressed but rather preserved by women's sharing in the diaconal ministry.

The deeper question at hand is arguably that of distinguishing the potentially variable, local practices of individual communities from that which the Church does and must hold in common. It is simpler to subscribe to the Vincentian Canon in principle, after all, than to specify exactly what has in fact been believed "everywhere, always and by all".[11] One sees this tension in full force in a recent exchange between two eminent North American Orthodox theologians, Paul Ladouceur and Father Lawrence Farley.[12] The debate does not centre on the nature of the historical evidence itself, which both take to be incontrovertible. Rather, the question is the theological significance of the evidence: what it tells us about the Church of the past and what it may legitimate for the Church today.

Farley, for his part, anticipates that a "restored" office will likely not correspond to its predecessor, the features of which are today effectively obsolete. Instead, "restoration" will impel an ambiguous and uncircumscribed process of development, leading ultimately to the ordination of women to the priesthood and/or episcopate. Ladouceur, for his part, is open to this very prospect (on the basis of arguments from theological anthropology, as articulated by notable figures in twentieth-century Orthodox theology), while Farley is categorically opposed—in part because such ordinations in other Churches have not infrequently been associated with a comprehensive revisiting of the catena of traditional approaches to gender and sexuality. Ladouceur's rejoinder is that such an objection amounts to a *"post hoc, propter hoc"* alarmism: no Orthodox dogma is at stake, but only customs that in and of themselves are not essential to Orthodoxy.

In conclusion, there is a growing sense among Eastern Christians that this debate is, and will continue to be, a bellwether of how their Churches will face other contemporary controversies which arguably are not related to it per se (i.e. which are not logical or necessary corollaries of it), but which nonetheless appear—on the basis of the experience of Western Christians—to have followed in its wake (for better or for worse!). Speaking pragmatically, the Eastern Catholic Churches will almost certainly wait to see what transpires in the Latin Church, in terms of how it ultimately responds to the results of the Study Commission on the Women's Diaconate established by Pope Francis in 2016. The Orthodox Churches, by contrast, will presumably continue to act somewhat independently (as, for instance, the Patriarchate of Alexandria and Greek Orthodox Church have each done thus far), all the while carefully monitoring and gauging the response of those with whom they are in communion. The decision to once again ordain women to the diaconate, and the concomitant discernment concerning the appropriate shape of their ministry in the present day, will one way or another prove of signal importance for the development of Eastern Christianity in the twenty-first century.

Notes

1   To date, the most comprehensive treatment of the issue from within the Orthodox world is the following edited collection, in which the more than three dozen authors, between themselves, reference the host of relevant primary and secondary literature: Petros Vassiliadis, Niki Papageorgiou, and Eleni Kasselouri-Hatzivassiliadi (eds), *Deaconesses, the Ordination of Women and Orthodox Theology* (Newcastle upon Tyne, UK: Cambridge Scholars Publishing, 2017).

2   See, for example, Kyriaki Karidoyanes Fitzgerald, *Women Deacons in the Orthodox Church: Called to Holiness and Ministry* (Brookline, MA: Holy Cross Press, 1998).

[3] Cited in Kyriaki Karidoyanes Fitzgerald (ed.), *Orthodox Women Speak: Discerning the "Signs of the Times"* (Geneva & Brookline, MA: WCC Publications & Holy Cross Orthodox Press, 1999), pp. 15–18.

[4] See "Orthodox Clergy and Laity Take Stand against Deaconesses" (15 January 2018). See <http://www.aoiusa.org/a-public-statement-on-orthodox-deaconesses-by-concerned-clergy-and-laity/> (accessed 1 October 2018). Fifty-seven clergymen and lay leaders, including heads of two Orthodox seminaries in the United States, issued a public statement calling on church leaders to "defend Orthodox teaching on the creation and calling of man as male and female by opposing the appointment of deaconesses in the Orthodox Church". They express explicit opposition to actions of the Patriarchate of Alexandria and the support given thereto by a small but influential group of Greek and American liturgists.

[5] The most accessible single resource remains Abel Oghlukian, *The Deaconess in the Armenian Church: A Brief Survey*, trans. and ed. S. Peter Cowe (New Rochelle, NY: St Nerses Armenian Seminary, 1994).

[6] Among her myriad publications, Phyllis Zagano—surely the world expert on the topic of women deacons—has carefully researched the intriguing precedent extant in the Maronite tradition, dating back to the Synod of Mount Lebanon (1736), which was responsible for the codification of that Church's canon law. Approved in *forma specifica* by Pope Benedict XIV in 1741 and never repealed—although its provisions on the matter at hand remain dormant, due to the non-existence of Maronite deaconesses at present—the synodal decrees reveal a modest liturgical role for the deaconess in the monastic context, apparently including even the (sacrament of the) anointing of the sick.

[7] See <https://armenianweekly.com/2018/01/16/historic-ordination-tehran-diocese-armenian-church-ordains-deaconess/> (accessed 1 October 2018).

[8] See the following book, to which I have contributed a chapter: Helena Kupari and Elina Vuola (eds), *Gender in Orthodox Christianity* (Abingdon: Routledge, 2019).

[9] Thus, the landmark 1988 Rhodes Consultation of Orthodox hierarchs and theologians, which treated "The Place of Women in the Orthodox Church and the Question of the Ordination of Women", calling for "the revival of this ancient order . . . on the basis of the ancient prototypes testified in so many sources". But the Consultation qualified that such a revival be also "in the

spirit of ancient tradition and in response to the increasing specific needs of our time": "[W]ould it not be possible and desirable to allow women to enter into the 'lower orders' through a blessing of the Church: sub-deacon, reader, cantor, teacher . . . without excluding new orders that the Church might consider to be necessary? This matter deserves further study since there is no definite tradition of this sort" (cited in Fitzgerald, *Women Deacons in the Orthodox Church*, p. 206).

[10] For instance, the report on the 2003 Oriental Orthodox and Roman Catholic Consultation observes: "The Coptic Church is now in the process of restoring the female diaconate in three orders: the female reader for women (now called 'devoted one'), sub-deaconess (now called 'assistant deaconess'), and deaconess. The Coptic Holy Synod has made it clear that deaconesses may not in any way participate in service of the altar or sacerdotal service . . . The rite of initiation into the female diaconate is performed by a bishop without the laying-on-of-hands but with a signing of the cross three times over the candidate. In their ministry they are to work exclusively with women and children. They assist at the baptism of women, visit sick women in hospitals, supervise women's activities in parishes, and clean the church building except for the sanctuary area which they may not enter." <http://sor.cua.edu/Ecumenism/20030626oorcconsultation.html> (accessed 1 October 2018). The Assyrian Church of the East, by contrast, allows for liturgical service, but only of a strictly defined sort: the branch of the Church in India, where it is known as the Chaldean Syrian Church, has three deaconesses currently serving, all over the age of fifty. They must be widows or nuns, and are employed exclusively in the context of adult baptisms, which are still performed according to the ancient manner, by the immersion of nude candidates (typically Hindu women converting in order to marry Christian men). No other liturgical ministry is envisioned at present, although at least one is active in catechesis.

[11] Vatican II referred to this dialectic in its decree on the Eastern Churches, *Orientalium Ecclesiarum* (1964): "[T]here exists an admirable bond of union, such that the variety within the Church in no way harms its unity; rather it manifests it, for it is the mind of the Catholic Church that each individual Church or Rite should retain its traditions whole and entire and likewise that it should adapt its way of life to the different needs of time and place" (2). The decree further affirms that all "should attain to an ever greater knowledge

and a more exact use of [their Rite and way of life] and, if in their regard they have fallen short owing to contingencies of times and persons, they should take steps to return to their ancestral traditions" (6). Available at <http:// www.vatican.va/archive/hist_councils/ii_vatican_council/documents/vat-ii_ decree_19641121_orientalium-ecclesiarum_en.html> (accessed 1 October 2018).

[12] For the latest instalment of the debate, rehearsing the earlier exchanges, see the following: Paul Ladouceur, "Christ, The Fathers and Feminism: Dialogue with Fr Lawrence Farley", *St Vladimir's Theological Quarterly* 62:3 (2018), pp. 287–295.

P A R T   4

Ecumenical Views of the Diaconate

CHAPTER 8

"To Minister and to Mediate": A Theological Consideration of the Diaconate in the Orthodox and Eastern Catholic Churches

Brian A. Butcher

Introduction

A variety of models informs the identity and ministry of deacons in the Eastern Churches; notable contrasts can be observed not only across the East and West Syrian, Armenian, Alexandrian and Byzantine traditions, but also between the contemporary Orthodox and Catholic ecclesial expressions of these traditions. What are the common features of the diaconal office in the Christian East? What in turn is the significance of the differences—especially when set in relationship to the diaconate as it has developed in the West? Proceeding from the particular to the general, let us canvass the distinctive shape of the diaconate in a number of the Eastern Churches, so as to in turn be able to consider their commonalities. An inductive approach will allow us to discern the general "Tradition" diffused amidst the extant "traditions".[1]

The one Church and the communion of the Churches

Eastern Christianity conventionally refers to several different streams of apostolic Churches, which today exist within four separate ecclesial communions: the Assyrian Church of the East, presently in full communion with no other Church; the Oriental Orthodox Churches; the Eastern Orthodox Church(es); and the Eastern-Rite Catholic Churches. These share a number of common features vis-à-vis Western forms of Christianity, even though they represent among themselves a rich variety of theological, liturgical, spiritual and canonical traditions, termed by John Paul II as that "genuine plurality of forms which remains the Church's ideal".[2]

The East Syrian tradition

The East Syrian tradition today comprises the much-beleaguered Assyrian Church of the East (400,000 members) as well as its Catholic counterpart, the Chaldean Catholic Church (419,000 members): both communities suffered dreadful persecution in the early twentieth century, and of course more recently, in their Mesopotamian homeland, especially present-day Iraq. Both in turn have witnessed a historically unprecedented emigration from the Middle East to the West, whether Western Europe, North America or Oceania. Also included in this tradition is the vibrant Syro-Malabar Catholic Church of Kerala, in southern India (3,903,000 members).

Traditionally, the various orders of the Church have been seen as corresponding to the angelic hierarchy, from the office of patriarch on down; there are nine ranks in each, with the lowest three (deacon, subdeacon, reader) comprising the diaconate. Deacons are matched to "principalities", while subdeacons correspond to archangels and readers to angels. Over the one to be ordained reader, the following prayer is read: "Make [him] worthy to be entrusted with the reading of the holy Scriptures and divine words before your chosen people in your holy Church. . .", while the bishop is advised thus in regard to subdeacons:

> You ought to know that readers and subdeacons are not to be
> signed on the forehead nor does the Spirit descend on them, but
> a special prayer is said which separates them from lay people for
> the closing of the doors, for service before the Levites, and for
> reading the prophetic books.

Here we have evidence of a common distinction in the Eastern
Churches between the so-called minor and major orders. Importantly,
and characteristically, the deacons are referred to as *Levites*, stressing at
once their *liturgical* role and, concomitantly, the continuity of Christian
liturgical service with the cult of the Old Testament; this is so, even as the
diaconate is recapitulated in the New Testament ministry of Stephen—a
corollary equally ubiquitous in the Christian East. Such a twofold origin
for the diaconate is highlighted in the prayer over the *ordinandi*:

> [You who] placed in [your holy Church] also pure deacons for
> the service of your glorious and holy mysteries; and as you chose
> Stephen and his companions, so now also, Lord, according to
> your mercy give to these your servants the grace of the Holy
> Spirit, that they may . . . serve at your pure altar with a clean heart
> and good conscience, and may shine in works of righteousness,
> serving at your life-giving and divine mysteries . . . Set apart,
> sanctified, perfected and complete is N. for the work of the
> diaconate in the Church, and for the execution of the Levitical
> and Stephanite office . . . [3]

The Assyrian Church of the East even today does not allow for the
celebration of the Eucharist by a presbyter alone, i.e. without a deacon
serving alongside; in this respect, as in many others, they preserve a
pattern once common across the Church.

The West Syrian tradition

Like its Eastern counterpart, the West Syrian tradition includes communities historically rooted in the Middle East, as well as a strong presence in India: the Syriac (also known as Jacobite) Orthodox Church (500,000 + 1,200,000 in India); the Syriac Catholic Church (175,000); the Malankara Orthodox Syrian Church (2,500,000); the Syro-Malankara Catholic Church (413,000); and the Maronite Catholic Church of Lebanon (3,106,000). And like their Assyrian brethren, the West Syrian Churches have traditionally used a form of the language spoken by Christ, namely Syriac, for both worship and scholarship.

The diaconate in these churches is variously itemized, with the following ranks being common:[4] chanter (*mzamrono*)—with those participating in the revived order of "deaconess" actually functioning as "chantresses"; reader (*quroyo*); subdeacon (*afudyaqno*); deacon (*mshamshono*); and archdeacon (an honorific designation). Due to past and present Latin influence, it has become common in Indian churches, whether Orthodox or Catholic, for traditional diaconal responsibilities to devolve upon unordained acolytes ("altar boys"—and, in at least some Syro-Malabar, Syriac Catholic, and Maronite parishes in the West, "altar girls"). Such receive a blessing and wear the alb (but no stole). In turn, the minor orders, and the full diaconate, serve usually as transitional states.

In the Syriac Orthodox churches of the Middle East, however, the minor orders survive, as well as full deacons. Notably, preaching may on occasion be entrusted to the lower ranks, as well as to laity, both men and women. This contemporary development is predicated on the idea that theological education, rather than ordination, is the most important factor in assigning the liturgical homily. Furthermore, today it has become common for any rank of deacon (or "acolyte") to fulfil responsibilities formerly reserved to the "full deacon", including swinging the censer (the incense, however, being blessed and imposed by the priest) and putting away the sacred vessels. It remains proper to a deacon or, in his absence, a priest, to read the Gospel and take Holy Communion to those absent.

A final point of interest, in light of the strict Byzantine tradition discussed below in which only *major* orders are conferred at the altar—a custom which contributes to maintaining a firm distinction between them and all other ranks—is that in the Syriac Orthodox Church today *all* ordinations occur at the altar and after the elevation of the Holy Mysteries during the Qurbono (alternatively referred to as Qurbana: "Offering" = Divine Liturgy). Candidates for the minor orders typically stand during the ordination rite, rather than kneel as the major orders do (diaconal ordinands on one knee, presbyteral ones on both). While this custom is strictly observed in the Syriac Orthodox Church, whether in the Middle East or India, the case is otherwise for the Malankara Orthodox Syrian Church, in which subdiaconal candidates, for example, may also be asked to kneel. Such a blurring of the line between the different grades of ministry is further displayed in the common practice, also found among the Copts, of using the term "deacon" to refer to anyone having received ordination to a rank below that of priest.

The Armenian tradition

The Armenian tradition is unique in its peculiar blend of Syriac, Byzantine and Latin elements, which have combined with those of local origin to produce both a strikingly rich liturgy and a markedly independent ecclesiological mindset. As discussed in my other contribution to the present volume, the Armenian Apostolic Church—the sole bearer, along with the much smaller Armenian Catholic Church, of the Armenian religious patrimony—is the maverick of the Christian East in regard to women deacons: it is only there that the office has enjoyed a relatively stable (if always marginal) ecclesiastical status, and only there that the diaconal ministry as such is practised in identical manner by those ordained to it, whether male or female.

Today, in the Armenian Apostolic Church, there are two minor orders: the combined office of acolyte/reader/porter, to which, in a few locales, girls may be ordained (before puberty); and that of subdeacon (*gisasargavak*), to which the functions of the deacon (*sargavak*) are commonly delegated. Such functions include censing, leading litanies, reading the Gospel during the Surp Badarak ("Holy Offering" = Divine Liturgy) and carrying the chalice in the Great Entrance. The prayer for the ordination of a deacon petitions thus:

> Give him the strength and grace of Stephen the apostle and first
> martyr, and first deacon and minister of your worship. To the end
> that, filled with the Holy Spirit, he may stand fast in the service
> of your holy altar, perfuming your Church with the incense of a
> sweet-smelling life and with exemplary good works. May he cause
> himself and all your servants, near and far, to rejoice.[5]

The Armenian Apostolic Church presently has many men who serve as
"permanent" (to use the Western terminology) deacons; women deacons
are necessarily so, since the Armenian Church, in concert with all other
Eastern Churches, both Catholic and Orthodox, does not ordain women
to the priesthood or episcopate. Unlike the Syriac Orthodox deacon, but
like his Byzantine counterpart, an Armenian deacon may lead a Liturgy of
the Word (*jashou*), as well as distribute Holy Communion in the absence
of a priest. And yet deacons do not habitually preach, as is often the
case among the Jacobites; where the laity *are* similarly permitted to do
so—again, in respect of theological training—the preaching must not
take place from the altar, i.e. the raised platform from which the liturgy
is conducted, only accessed by those ordained.

Interestingly, although Armenian canon law forbids deacons to marry
after ordination, this practice has in fact become common over the past
century-and-a-half, whether in Armenia itself or abroad. This trend is
arguably expressive of the characteristic Eastern practice of *oikonomia*,
i.e. the episcopal prerogative to mitigate canonical strictures in individual
cases, in favour of the spiritual welfare of the parties concerned. The
Ethiopian and Eritrean Churches allow deacons to marry in any case, as
do the Assyrians (for whom marriage is permissible even after presbyteral
ordination). Coptic, Jacobite and Byzantine deacons, on the other hand,
must embrace either marriage or celibacy *prior* to diaconal ordination
and are canonically obliged to remain in their chosen state.

The Alexandrian tradition

The Coptic Orthodox Church of Alexandria today numbers between fifteen and eighteen million faithful and has in recent decades established a dynamic presence across the globe. In a few places outside Egypt, one may also find communities of the much smaller Coptic Catholic Church (197,000). Increasing numbers of Copts are emigrating from Egypt every year, not least because of the ongoing, if only occasionally conspicuous, discrimination and persecution to which they are subject, within a contemporary Islamic context marked by radicalist tendencies. The Coptic Church is part of the Oriental Orthodox family, that is, those churches which did not receive the Council of Chalcedon—regarded as the Fourth Ecumenical Council by Catholics and Eastern Orthodox alike; today they are often referred to as non- or pre-Chalcedonian, or again as Miaphysite (in reference to their distinctive Christology).

One of the first things any visitor to a Coptic church will notice is the vast number of boys, often very young, and men, vested in alb and stole at the front left (or both left and right, in two choirs) of the church, in an area known as the "first chancel" or *psalteria*. These are habitually called "deacons", although they in fact represent an array of the minor orders; only rarely will any of them be a full deacon. Interestingly, approved and recognized lay ministers (both male and female), i.e. those who lead catechism or execute other, non-liturgical functions in Coptic parish life, are typically referred to as "servants".

There are five ranks of deacon in Coptic practice today: chanter (*epsaltos*), reader (*anagnostes*), subdeacon (*epidiakon*), deacon and archdeacon. Only the full diaconate is seen as "the first and the least rank in the priesthood"; those in lower orders, nonetheless, are still considered clergy, other than the chanters (who are deemed laymen). While Copts have in recent decades begun consecrating women as deaconesses, these are rather what would be termed apostolic women religious in the West; such deaconesses may not enter the altar area, even to clean it (except in the case of convent chapels), nor do they typically read the scriptures or fulfil any other official liturgical roles.

The distinctive characteristics of the (male) diaconate among the Copts include ordaining chanters as young as six years old (while a reader may be ordained at sixteen, a subdeacon at twenty, and a deacon at twenty-five).[6] Ordination is at the door of the altar, but with the candidate standing in the *psalteria*, in all cases, and ordination always occurs in between the Liturgy of the Catechumens and the Liturgy of the Faithful, after the "Prayer of Reconciliation" and before the Kiss of Peace. Despite the similarity of the rites thus far, hands are not laid on any but those to be ordained full deacon, who alone may assist with the distribution of Holy Communion—and even then, only of the Precious Blood. In his absence, the administration of the Eucharist is done exclusively by the priest, regardless of how this may in turn prolong the service. By contrast, the other, properly diaconal duties are customarily assumed by the lesser ranks—even, for example, the reading of the Gospel.

Copts do routinely lament the erosion of the diaconal ministry in their Church (i.e. the relegation of authentically diaconal tasks to minor clerics), as well as the relative scarcity of full deacons: apparently due to the canonical prohibition on having secular employment, they are rarely ordained except as a step toward priesthood. And yet there are exceptions: an increasing number of permanent deacons are to be found in the United States particularly, as well as in certain dioceses of Egypt.

The traditional understanding of the diaconate, which includes an emphasis on the corporal works of mercy, is expressed in the impressive exhortation directed to the ordinand:

> The work of ministry with which you have been entrusted, O my
> son, is great. It is necessary for you, therefore, to fulfil those things
> which have been assigned for you to do, since you have been
> enrolled as a son of Stephen, the first deacon: to visit the people
> of the Lord, the widows and the orphans and the afflicted. You
> shall gladden those whom you are able to help and supply their
> needs, being an example for them so that they might see your
> good works and emulate them from your behaviour; following
> the bishop or the presbyter, informing him about the afflicted, so
> that he might visit them . . . Know, therefore, the measure of the
> honour which has been given you and bear it, which is the true
> blood which was given for the salvation of the world, which was
> given into your hands . . . [7]

Finally, it is noteworthy that the Coptic Church, like the East Syrian tradition described above, diligently preserves a sense of continuity between the Old and New Covenants. This is evident not only in the already-stated prohibition of women from the altar but also in the *propitiatory* use of incense: because incense is thought of as first and foremost sacrificial rather than simply honorific, the thurible is never swung even by a deacon—the sole exception being the monastic deacons who serve in Jerusalem's Church of the Holy Sepulchre—much less by those in the minor orders.

Historically linked to the Coptic Church, due to its dependency upon the Patriarchate of Alexandria, is the Ethiopian Orthodox Tewahedo Church, which today numbers over forty-five million. The patrimony of this Church is also found within its much smaller Catholic counterpart, as well as the Eritrean Orthodox Tewahedo ("Tewahdo") Church (1,700,000) and the only-recently (2015) established Eritrean Catholic Church (158,480). Since its bishops came from Alexandria until the twentieth century (the first native bishops being consecrated in 1928), the Ethiopian Church has come to possess ordination rites effectively identical to those of the Copts; in practice, however, there are several intriguing differences in how their respective diaconates function.

Most surprising, perhaps, is that in Ethiopian practice lower orders—namely, chanter, reader and subdeacon—are even today bundled with the diaconal ordination, such that pre-pubescent boys find themselves serving as full deacons. This relates at least in part to the stricture that no Divine Liturgy may be celebrated without at least one deacon assisting: the norm, in fact, is to have two priests and three deacons. Ironically, there are very few active deacons to be found among older men (the demographic where, precisely, they *are* to be found among the Copts). Instead, by around the age of thirty, most deacons will have pursued one of a number of other ecclesiastical vocations: becoming a priest; pursuing monastic life; attaining one of two *sui generis* offices of liturgical expert (*marigeta*) or renowned catechist (*memher*); or "retiring" to the laity. Some do proceed to the effectively honorific rank of archdeacon. Differing from Coptic practice, Ethiopian deacons not only may but *must* distribute the Precious Blood: this falls to them even in the presence of additional priests, as does the task (in certain communities) of bringing up infants to receive the Holy Gifts. Conversely, however, while they are permitted to proclaim the Pauline and Catholic Epistles and Acts of the Apostles—a selection from each of which features in any Alexandrian-Rite Liturgy—the Gospel remains reserved to a priest.

The Byzantine tradition

Finally, we come to the Byzantine tradition, represented by what is today the most multicultural and demographically significant body of Eastern Christians, the (Eastern) Orthodox Church(es), as well as their invariably smaller Greek (or Greco-) Catholic "Sister Churches", of which there are fourteen. There are two to three minor orders in use in the Byzantine-Rite Churches today, despite there having been a number of additional offices in times past.

In the Slavic tradition, a man may be made a candle-bearer before receiving clerical tonsure—marked by a prayer indicating that he has now entered into the service of the Church. Subsequently, he is ordained to an office which is alternately understood as that of reader or cantor; the candidate who aspires to be recognized and function as a reader demonstrates his skill by proclaiming a portion from the lectionary, while a cantor undertakes the singing of a psalm (specifically, a *prokeimenon*). This rite has traditionally been seen as the "first degree of the priesthood". The second degree is that of the subdiaconate. The bishop prays over the candidate thus:

> [G]rant him to love the beauty of your house, to stand at the doors of your holy temple, to light the lamps of the dwelling of your glory; and plant him in your holy church like a fruitful olive tree, bringing forth fruit of righteousness, and make your servant perfect, in the time of your appearing . . . .[8]

Ordination to this office, as to those preceding it, always happens outside the altar area and usually not within the context of the Divine Liturgy.

By contrast, the Byzantine deacon is ordained after the anaphora, just prior to the distribution of Communion: this is taken to signify his primary role, namely to assist the bishop in the celebration of the Eucharist, as a servant at the Table. On a related note, he is entrusted with a liturgical fan (*rapidion*), which he will henceforth wave over the Gifts (during the anaphora), an action which, while having an obvious practical significance in certain climates, now denotes the "angelic" vocation of the deacon. The ordination formula correspondingly declares: "The divine grace, which always heals that which is infirm and supplies what is lacking, appoints the [subdeacon] N . . . as [deacon] . . . ."[9]

As in the other Eastern traditions, the Byzantine diaconate is typically regarded as a grade of priesthood (*hierosyne*). Focus is equally on service to God *with* the bishop (*latreuin*), as well as service *on behalf of* him (*doulein*). The most penetrating reflection on this peculiar dual character of the diaconate is arguably the recent book by Greek Orthodox deacon John Chryssavgis, *Diakonia*, which has inspired the title of this chapter. A seasoned deacon and prolific theologian, Chryssavgis offers the mature fruit of a lifetime of both serving in, and reflecting upon, the mystery of his order. As he writes:

> More perhaps than any other order of the ordained clergy—or at least more *apparently* than any other order of the ordained clergy—the deacon is both minister and mediator: minister before the altar of God and to the people of God: mediator between the heavenly altar and the earthly reality. The deacon appears to have one foot in heaven and one on earth, functioning in two worlds simultaneously, as well as bringing or holding together two different realities . . . [T]he deacon's responsibility is twofold; he leads the laity in prayer, urging them to bow their heads or offer supplication. However, he also addresses the celebrant clergy in liturgy, inviting them to commence a particular segment or make a certain gesture.[10]

Despite the prominence of the deacon in Byzantine liturgical services, the ritual tradition also displays a curiously subversive ambivalence with respect to the clerical status of the deacon: this is manifest in the inexplicable practice (shared by the Armenians) of according deacons the funeral service appointed for a layman.[11] Priests, by contrast, and even monastics (male and female), are buried with a distinct rite. More coherently, the West Syrian as well as the Coptic liturgical traditions include a diaconal funeral service, as well as forms proper to the presbyteral and monastic ranks just mentioned.

In the context of the present volume, in which other essays treat the diaconate in its Anglican and Roman Catholic expressions (and its Methodist and Lutheran forms too), it is perhaps important at this point to add that the Eastern deacon invariably ministers, as Chryssavgis indicates, *with* and *unto* the presiding clergy, as well as the faithful. While this is, of course, the historic Western practice as well, it is a commonplace that in recent decades Roman Catholic deacons, for example, have routinely come to be the principal celebrant of certain rites, in the absence of a presbyter/bishop (particularly baptisms, marriages and funerals). No equivalent idea (or practice) obtains in the Christian East: that is, a deacon is not regarded as the "ordinary" minister of any of the sacraments, in the sense of being able to *preside*, but only ever an assistant in the responsibilities of another: he is a servant of the Mysteries rather than a steward.

There remains much work to be done to renew the received forms of diaconal ministry in all the churches, even as this process itself invariably raises a number of further challenges. In any event, all will surely agree that knowledge of the diversity displayed in the Christian East in the past (and indeed the present!) serves at the very least to extend our imagination—imagination being a necessary, if not quite a sufficient, condition for discernment for the future.

Notes

[1]   A series of interviews with Eastern Christian deacons or diaconal candidates undergirds this chapter: special thanks go to Subdeacon Pradeep Hatcher of the Malankara Orthodox Syrian Church; Deacon Ryan Tellalian of the Armenian Apostolic Church; Andrew N. Abdelmalek, a chanter in the Coptic Orthodox Church; and diaconal candidate Augustine Dickinson of the Ethiopian Orthodox Tewahedo Church.

2   *Orientale lumen* §2. Available at <https://w2.vatican.va/content/john-paul-ii/
    en/apost_letters/1995/documents/hf_jp-ii_apl_19950502_orientale-lumen.
    html> (accessed 1 October 2018). For a full itemization of the various Eastern
    Churches, see Ronald Roberson, *The Eastern Christian Churches: A Brief
    Survey [7th Edition]* (Rome: Edizioni "Orientalia Christiana", 2008). See also
    my "Orthodox Tradition", in George Thomas Kurian and Mark A. Lamport
    (eds), *Encyclopedia of Christianity in the United States*, vol. 4: N–S (London:
    Rowman & Littlefield, 2016), pp. 1711–1718.

3   Paul Bradshaw, *Ordination Rites of the Ancient Churches of East and West*
    (Collegeville: Liturgical Press, 1990), p. 159. Bradshaw provides the most
    accessible and comprehensive collection of ordination rites for the different
    Eastern traditions. For extensive commentary on the material presented in
    this volume, see his later *Rites of Ordination: Their History and Theology*
    (Collegeville, MN: Liturgical Press, 2013).

4   Some lists include all the baptized faithful as an order (*'ulmoyo*); the Syro-
    Malankara in turn preserve a subsequent rank of Confessor of the Faith
    (*mawdyono*).

5   Bradshaw, *Ordination Rites of the Ancient Churches of East and West*, pp.
    128–129.

6   For an overview of Coptic practices concerning the diaconate, see <https://
    www.stmarystmark.ca/download/hgsd/DeaconshipRanksResponsibilities
    andOrdinationGuidelines.pdf> (accessed 1 October 2018).

7   Bradshaw, *Ordination Rites of the Ancient Churches of East and West*, pp.
    144–145.

8   Ibid., p. 139.

9   Ibid., pp. 133, 136.

10 John Chryssavgis, *Diakonia* (Brookline, MA: Holy Cross Orthodox Press,
    2009), pp. 107–108.

11 An example of what Chryssavgis means in saying the following: "[T]he
    office of the deacon is twofold, for the deacon is both clergy and laity—or,
    perhaps more accurately, the deacon is neither. He sometimes is not clearly
    identified with the ordained clergy; and he certainly cannot be identified with
    the unordained laity" (*Diakonia*, p. 108).

CHAPTER 9

The British Methodist Diaconal Order: Medium and Message

David Clark

Some years ago, Ernst Schumacher wrote a still-famous book entitled *Small is Beautiful*.[1] That phrase well describes the British Methodist Diaconal Order. In 2018, it had only 127 active deacons (full-time and paid), nine deacons in training and 118 retired deacons (though many are still very much engaged in diaconal ministry). However, the Methodist Diaconal Order (MDO) continues to punch well above its weight on the British church scene and embraces many of the hallmarks of what is now being called "a renewed diaconate". In this chapter, I sketch out why this is so. However, first I provide a short history.

A brief history

In 1869, the Revd Thomas Bowman Stephenson, a Wesleyan minister, founded the Children's Home (later called the National Children's Home and Orphanage and, more recently, Action for Children) to meet the needs of many destitute children in the burgeoning cities of the Industrial Revolution. He was greatly influenced by the initiative of Pastor Theodore Fliedner, the founder of a Lutheran deaconess community in 1836 in Kaiserswerth, Germany. In 1878, Bowman Stephenson recruited single women to work for the Children's Home as Sisters of the Children. This development triggered the idea of an order of women employed in three main fields: moral and spiritual education; ministry to the sick poor; and evangelism.

It was not long before the United Methodist Church and the Primitive Methodist Church set up similar associations of sisters or deaconesses. The work developed rapidly. In 1901, the Wesleyan deaconesses were officially "recognized" as a distinctive form of lay ministry by the Wesleyan Methodist Conference. In 1902, a Wesley Deaconess Institute was founded in Ilkley, Yorkshire, to provide accommodation and training facilities for twenty-seven students. By 1907, there were ninety-eight fully trained Wesleyan deaconesses, fifty-six probationers and nineteen accepted for training.[2]

To support the apostolate of the Wesley Deaconess Order, Bowman Stephenson fostered their life as a religious community. He set down three principles which in time became a classic frame of reference for the Order:[3]

- There should be vocation but no vow . . .
- There should be discipline but not servility . . .
- There should be association, but it should not exclude freedom . . .

However, in time all the different Methodist associations of deaconesses adopted some form of collective discipline and came to regard themselves as religious communities.

The year 1932 saw the union of Wesleyan Methodism, the United Methodist Church, and Primitive Methodism. Within two years, the deaconess associations of all these remaining branches of Methodism came together under the title of the Wesley Deaconess Order. Overall, this then had a membership of some 370 deaconesses.[4]

The post-World War II years saw considerable fluctuations in the life and work of the Wesley Deaconess Order. Its rule of life remained consistently strong. From 1963 onwards, deaconesses who married were permitted to remain in the Order. However, its apostolate was greatly influenced by the coming of the Welfare State, not least a National Health Service, a universal education system and increasing affluence. Its ministry of "witness through service" was increasingly taken over by secular professions and deaconesses found themselves becoming jacks-of-all-trades. The decision by the Methodist Church to ordain women to presbyteral ministry from 1974 meant yet another challenge to the survival of the Order. As a result, in 1978, the British Methodist Conference decided to end recruitment to the Order.

However, Methodism was taken by surprise when the idea of a religious order with an apostolate to address the changing needs of the wider world continued to retain its resilience. Thus, in 1986, the Methodist Conference agreed to the reopening of what, after 1988, was called "the Methodist Diaconal Order" (MDO), now embracing men and women. In 1987, the first deacons were ordained into that Order. In 1993, the Methodist Conference recognized the MDO as an order of ministry and a religious order, thus acknowledging its historic continuity with the Wesley Deaconess Order. All deacons were received into "Full Connexion"[5] in 1998. In 2004, the Methodist Conference took the report *What is a Deacon?*[6] to be the accepted understanding of the life and work of the MDO at that time.

Servant leadership

I have argued elsewhere[7] that the Church of the future has to become the servant of what I call "the kingdom community". That relationship means that it is fundamentally a servant, or "diaconal", Church, with an ecclesiology, including that of a renewed diaconate, to match that designation. The Methodist Church retains many characteristics of the diaconal church. For example, as stated in its original *Deed of Union*,[8] the Methodist Church upholds the principle that the ministries of laity, presbyter and deacon are of equal standing. This conviction reflects a key ecclesiological characteristic of the diaconal Church—that of every member being engaged in servant ministry and those appointed to positions of authority exercising servant leadership.

However, the MDO goes further and embraces a vision of a new model of servant leadership—that of being not only an order of ministry, but an order of *mission*. This means moving away from an apostolate focused on "witness through service", the normative calling of deacons over the past century or more, to assume the role and responsibilities of "mission enablers", encouraging and equipping the people of God to be the Church dispersed in the world. What makes the diaconal role of mission enabler so important is that the institutional Church, especially in the West, remains stuck in the mould of Christendom. In particular, clericalism still dominates the scene and the ministry of lay people, as the Church's primary mission resource, remains under-developed. A renewed diaconate is being called out to take on the leadership role of mission enabler to help equip the people of God to exercise their ministry in a world fundamentally different from that of Christendom.

What is Deacon?[9] reflects this change of focus. It states that "the primary purpose" of diaconal ministry is "to help all Christians discover, develop and express their own servant ministry. Deacons therefore engage in educational and nurturing activities to enable people to see God's activity in daily life and world, and encourage them in expressing their faith in relevant ways."

In 2008, Sue Jackson, a former Warden of the MDO, wrote:

> I believe that we are dealing with the need for a Copernican shift in people's understanding of diaconal leadership. All of us have to move from focusing on deacons as the prime agents of diaconal ministry to lay people as the crucial servants, assisted by deacons. This is as much a matter of attitudinal change in deacons themselves as in the church generally—though it does not follow a clear developmental pattern. Thus I believe that we need to attend primarily to the matter of attitude when thinking about the factors that hinder or help deacons become enablers, although I do not want to underestimate the importance of structural issues or training.[10]

An unofficial "mission statement", widely appreciated within the Order when it was introduced in 2009 by another former Warden, describes the MDO as "a mission-focused, pioneering religious community committed to *enabling* [my italics] outreach, evangelism and service in God's world".

Community

The diaconal church is the servant of the kingdom community. I have described the latter's gifts as life, liberation, love and learning.[11] Thus the mission of the diaconal church is to help human collectives of all kinds—families, neighbourhoods, associations, institutions, cities[12] and nations—manifest the gifts of the kingdom community. But what does the kingdom community and its gifts look like?

I believe that British Methodism possesses a number of attributes which embody the gifts of the kingdom community. For example, it retains many features of its origins as a holiness movement,[13] with the kingdom community's gifts of life, liberation, love, and learning being to the fore. It is a profoundly communal church, with a strong emphasis on "fellowship" and pastoral care. It is a mutually supportive "Connexion".[14] Its annual elected Conference, consisting of presbyters, deacons and lay people, pursues a democratic form of decision-making. However, the MDO, as a religious order, is in a key position to model and express the gifts of the kingdom community even more fully—the medium here becomes the message.

Since it reopened in 1986, and from then on included women and men, the MDO has worked hard at enriching its life as a community. It has adopted a rule of life "to deepen (its) fellowship and bind (it) together as a dispersed community".[15] Its rule runs as follows:

Devotional Life
We endeavour to:

- Attend worship regularly, especially Holy Communion.
- Set aside time each day to read the Bible devotionally and to pray, including a time of intercession for members of the Order.
- Regularly set aside time for self-examination, a chance to look back and see where we have failed in loving God and our neighbours and to give thanks for blessings received.
- Find a spiritual director/companion who will accompany, help and affirm us, and make time each year for a retreat or quiet day.

Discipline

We endeavour to:

- Be sensitive to the needs of those close to us, our families, dependants and friends.
- Be aware of and relate to the community in which we live.
- Acknowledge and enjoy God's gifts to us of time, talents, money and possessions, and through God's grace be able stewards of these.
- Order the rhythm of each day, month and year to allow for study and relaxation, a weekly day off, and regular holidays.
- Attend Convocation (unless a dispensation is granted).
- Keep in contact with other members of the Order by the giving or receiving of fellowship and support, by visits and by letter or telephone (and now through the internet).

The gifts of the kingdom community—life, liberation, love, and learning—are exemplified in the life and work of the MDO in many of the attitudes and commitments mentioned above. I have explored these communal features of the life of the MDO more fully elsewhere.[16] Here I add two others. Reflecting the gift of liberation, every member of the MDO is treated as unique and of similar worth. The gifts and experience of student deacons in training, active deacons and retired deacons are constantly affirmed and their contributions to the life of church and world treated as equally significant. Reflecting the gift of love, the MDO publishes a *Daily Prayer Diary* each year in which appears the name, photograph, location and short prayer request of every deacon. This enables the whole Order to pray for the needs of every member of the Order on at least three occasions annually.

Intertwined

What is a Deacon? insists that the life and work of the MDO as an order of ministry, on the one hand, and a religious order, on the other, are "completely intertwined".[17] It is this "complete intertwining" that enables the MDO to model how the people of God might live out their calling to be kingdom community builders in every sphere of the life of society—be that in family life, education, health and welfare, law and order, finance and business, or administration and government. I believe that this exemplification of what it means to be a renewed diaconate, albeit by a small Order, is a vital contribution not only to Methodism, but to the universal Church to come, the diaconal Church.

Challenges

It would be naïve to assume that the MDO is moving swiftly and serenely forward in its journey towards becoming a renewed diaconate. In reality, it faces challenges from both within and beyond the Order. Within the Order, there are many who remain deeply committed to "witness through service" as the deacon's primary calling, rather than it now being that of enablers of the ministry of the people of God in the world. Nor does their training as yet equip deacons with the skills and experience required to undertake the difficult task of facilitating the ministry and mission of others.

A long heritage of being subject to male clericalism (the Warden of the Order was always a male presbyter until it was re-opened in 1986) has meant that many deacons fail to grasp that they are "a full and equal order"[18] alongside presbyters. Thus they find it difficult to accept with confidence and exercise the kind of leadership role which is so urgently needed by the Church in today's world. These challenges are exacerbated by the fact that British Methodism, alongside many other churches, is only just beginning to recognize the nature and potential of a renewed diaconate. One Methodist commentator on the MDO describes it as "Methodism's best kept secret" and another as "yeast in the dough of Methodism".[19] However, both comments indicate a church not fully aware of the treasure it possesses.

In 2013, the British Methodist Conference, perhaps cognisant that it needed to get to grips more fully with the potential of its diaconal order, set up a review "to undertake work on the theology and ecclesiology underpinning the Methodist Diaconal Order, its place within the British

Connexion and its place within the universal church". However, the report back to the Methodist Conference on this brief was very slow in coming and has now been postponed until 2019. In the meantime, a recent report proposing the interchangeability of presbyteral ministries between the Methodist Church and the Church of England appeared without addressing the place of the diaconates of either denomination in this important development.[20]

Nevertheless, it is my conviction that the emergence of a renewed diaconate within British Methodism and well beyond is a divine imperative. I believe it is a gift which will not only bring a radically new understanding of the nature and form of ordained leadership, diaconal *and* presbyteral, but, in time, be instrumental in transforming the Church to come into a diaconal Church.

Notes

[1]   E. F. Schumacher, *Small is Beautiful: A Study of Economics as if People Mattered* (London: Blond & Briggs, 1973).

[2]   J. M. Lloyd, *Women and the Shaping of British Methodism: Persistent Preachers, 1807–1907* (Manchester and New York: Manchester University Press, 2010), p. 249.

[3]   E. D. Graham, *Saved to Serve. The Story of the Wesley Deaconess Order, 1890–1978* (Peterborough: Methodist Publishing House, 2002), p. 241.

[4]   Ibid., p. 353.

[5]   Ecclesiologically, the Methodist Church regards itself as a communal body made up of an extended network of districts, circuits, local churches, and related groups and organizations, which make up what it calls "the Connexion". Oversight and authority lie with its annual Conference, an elected body consisting of presbyters, deacons and laity. When presbyters and deacons are ordained, they are also "received into Full Connexion".

[6]   *What is a Deacon?* Methodist Conference Report (2004).

[7]   D. Clark, *Breaking the Mould of Christendom: Kingdom Community, Diaconal Church and the Liberation of the Laity* (Peterborough: Upfront Publishing, 2005; reprinted 2014); D. Clark, (ed.), *The Diaconal Church: Beyond the Mould of Christendom* (Peterborough: Upfront Publishing, 2008; reprinted

2017); D. Clark, *Building Kingdom Communities: With the Diaconate as a New Order of Mission* (Peterborough: Fast-print Publishing, 2016).

8   *The Methodist Deed of Union* (1932), Section 2, Clause 4.

9   *What is a Deacon?* para. 5.4.

10   Clark, *Diaconal Church*, p. 162.

11   Clark, *Building Kingdom Communities*, pp. 12–18.

12   D. Clark, *Building the Human City—the Origins and Future Potential of the Human City Institute (1995–2002)* (2012—download from <http://www.humancity.org.uk>).

13   Clark, *Building Kingdom Communities*, pp. 162–168.

14   See note 5 above.

15   <https://www.methodistdiaconalorder.org.uk/index.php?page=rule-of-life>.

16   Clark, *Building Kingdom Communities*, pp. 178–184.

17   *What is a Deacon?* para. 3.5.

18   J. M. Barnett, *The Diaconate: A Full and Equal Order*, revised edition (Harrisburg, PA: Trinity Press International, 1995).

19   *Who do you say we are?* (London: Methodist Publishing, 2010–2011), paras. 6 and 15.

20   <https://www.churchofengland.org/sites/default/files/2017-10/mission-and-ministry-in-covenant.pdf>. See also my comments on this report in D. Clark, *The Gift of a Renewed Diaconate—and the Contribution of British Methodism* (Peterborough: Fast-print, 2018), pp. 123–138.

CHAPTER 10

Diaconates—the Lutheran Experience

*Anne Keffer and E. Louise Williams**

Diakonia and the Lutheran World Federation

Within the Lutheran World Federation (LWF), as in the World Council of Churches (WCC), *diakonia* is the term used for a wide variety of ministry, ranging from individual care of people in congregations to health and social service institutions to international aid and development. Much of the LWF's consulting and theologizing over the years has been about diaconal work and not about the diaconate as such. There are, of course, implications for the diaconates arising from the discussions of the theology and practice of *diakonia* as understood by the LWF. Below are described the three most recent documents.

1. The LWF convened a group in 2002 around the theme "Prophetic Diakonia—For the Healing of the World". The consultation

---

* We have chosen to write in a somewhat simplified form without endnotes, since most of what we write comes from years of personal study, private conversations, our own involvement on various committees and taskforces, and our participation and leadership in our own diaconates, church bodies, and ecumenical organizations. Additionally, neither of us is fluent in languages other than English. This means we have often worked with secondary sources and documents in translation. Because there is often a time lag before documents are available in English, some of the information may not represent the most recent decisions and activities of diaconates around the world.

focused on three specific areas of human suffering—poverty, violence and HIV/AIDS. Participants developed a letter to the churches of the LWF which spoke directly to those three areas as well as to *diakonia* in general. The heart of that letter begins:

> *Diakonia* is central to what it means to be the Church. As a core component of the gospel, *diakonia* is not an option but an essential part of discipleship. *Diakonia* reaches out to all persons, who are created in God's image. While *diakonia* begins as unconditional service to the neighbour in need, it leads inevitably to social change that restores, reforms and transforms.

The statement asserts that this *diakonia* is the calling of the whole people of God. It expresses the importance of leadership for *diakonia* in the churches and encourages incorporating deacons/diaconal ministers/deaconesses in "the Church's ordained, consecrated and commissioned ministries, as a reflection of the fundamental significance of *diakonia* for the being of the Church".

2. *The Diaconal Ministry in the Mission of the Church* was a consultation convened by the LWF in 2005. The purpose and intent of the consultation was to look at existing models of ordering diaconal ministry and to try to set parameters for demarcating a "space" where diaconal ministry can be located within the overall ministry of the Church. They began with the assumption that, however that "space" might be understood, it should be:

- solidly based on the gospel as testified in the Bible;
- accountable to and informed by basic tenets of the Lutheran Reformation;
- open to contextual variations.

The final statement of the consultation advocates for ordaining those called to the ministry of *diakonia* as a way of demonstrating that the diaconate is an integral part of the one (public) ministry of the Church. At the same time, the statement affirms the "deaconhood of all believers", that is, the calling of all the baptized to be involved in *diakonia*. It also points to the importance of seeing the diaconal and pastoral ministries as mutual and complementary while having different emphases.

3. In 2009, drawing on these two consultations, the LWF published *Diakonia in Context: Transformation, Reconciliation, Empowerment—An LWF Contribution to the Understanding and Practice of Diakonia*. While the main focus of the document is the Church's diaconal mission expressed in many different ways and carried out by a variety of people, it also takes up the matter of ordering the Church's public ministry. It advocates for churches to re-examine how they order ministry and to include the diaconate in their public expression of ministry in ways that are appropriate for their context.

A bit of history

Many Lutheran diaconates around the world trace their roots to nineteenth-century Germany, where the advent of the Industrial Revolution and the end of the Napoleonic Wars left society in upheaval. The wars had left many women widowed and children orphaned without means of support. Additionally, many young women were left without prospect of marriage, because so many young men were killed at war. The Industrial Revolution triggered movement to the cities from the small towns and agricultural areas and resulted in poverty, unemployment, family breakdown, rapid spread of disease and other social ills. The guilds disintegrated and people lost the mutual support they provided. Urban families could no longer depend on their extended families and neighbours for care of children and family members who were ill or elderly. The Church, once central in the lives of people in villages and towns, became disconnected from people crowded together in the centres of large cities.

Into this milieu, two German Lutherans—Johann Hinrich Wichern, a layman, and Theodor Fliedner, a pastor—began to envision a programme of social action and evangelism called *Innere Mission*. (This was to complement the Church's foreign mission, which was flourishing in this time of nationalism and colonization.) The vision was to respond to some of the social problems in the cities and at the same time bring the gospel and a deeper spirituality to the lives of people.

Wichern, in 1833, first established houses for boys orphaned by the wars or neglected by families caught in the long hours of factory work. He set up family-type group homes with a surrogate older brother, *Bruder*, later called deacon. Wichern and his successors set up training programmes for deacons to work in jails, slums and other places of need. Wichern's work received approval from the church conference in Wittenberg in 1848 and grew with the Church's blessing.

Fliedner was a pastor in Kaiserswerth in an area where Lutherans were in the minority and where the Industrial Revolution flourished because of the proximity to the Rhine River and its shipping possibilities. On a trip to England to raise support for his congregation, Fliedner became acquainted with the work of Elizabeth Fry, an activist in prison work and reform. Dovetailing with the concept of the Inner Mission, Fliedner and his wife Friederike opened a halfway house for women prisoners in 1833. This was the first of many other "Fliedner" institutions that responded to the needs of those who were poor and marginalized. In an ingenious way, the Fliedners combined the needs of the poor with the need for status and support of the many unmarried young women to develop an approach to ministry that continues to this day.

In time, Theodor and Friederike Fliedner recruited young women to become deaconesses, living together as sisters in a motherhouse and becoming trained to serve as nurses, teachers, counsellors, and other workers in schools, hospitals, halfway houses, hospices, etc. Although Theodor was a Lutheran pastor, he chose to organize his deaconess houses and the institutions they staffed outside the official church structures. Initially, the women did not take life-long vows but agreed to serve for five-year periods. They lived a common life, receiving no salary, only pocket money. They followed a strict routine of morning and evening prayer, long hours of work, and quiet times for meditation and devotion. They wore the dress of married women of their day, giving them status in the community. As long as they were affiliated with the sisterhood, they were promised a place to be in illness or old age.

In a very few years, deaconesses from Kaiserswerth were serving in hospitals and other institutions around the world. Deaconess houses after the Kaiserswerth model sprang up throughout Germany and other European countries where Protestant (especially Lutheran) Christians were found. By 1864, the Kaiserswerth community had grown to 425 deaconesses and by 1894 there were 9,000 Lutheran deaconesses throughout the world. Motherhouses were formed in the Americas, Africa and Asia and eventually organized into the Kaiserswerth General Conference, an association that continues today.

Germany

Today in Germany, the direct descendants of Wichern's brotherhoods are called deacons. They are now officially commissioned by the Church, and both men and women can belong to their association. They rarely serve a liturgical function and continue to serve in a variety of social service agencies, often in leading positions as administrators and managers. Perhaps the reluctance of the German churches to utilize deacons liturgically is rooted in Martin Luther's opinions expressed in opposition to what he considered the abuse in the Roman Catholic Church, where deacons had liturgical duties but ignored the needs of the poor.

Approximately seventy motherhouses in Germany are part of the Kaiserswerth Verband, an association of communities from around the world rooted in Fliedner's model. A few groups continue to follow the original Kaiserswerth rule, including the traditional garb. Most of these groups have become sisterhoods of ageing and retired deaconesses, who fill the institutions which once served the larger community. They have become communities of prayer and support rather than communities of active workers. Other groups have made changes in their understanding of their orders or communities. While they maintain a sense of community and connection to the original motherhouse, they no longer live a common life. They may marry. They receive salaries for their work and make contributions back to their motherhouse. They are not expected to wear the traditional garb but are identified with a special pin or insignia. Usually the rite of entrance to these sisterhoods or communities is consecration. Within the communities, however, members may also choose to become ordained deacons or even ordained pastors.

Northern Europe

In Denmark, Finland, Norway and Sweden there were diaconates from the mid-1800s rooted in the model of the Kaiserswerth motherhouse. In addition, in Norway there was a "fatherhouse" for training male deacons.

Stimulated by the WCC's publication of *Baptism, Eucharist and Ministry* and spurred on by the ensuing ecumenical dialogues, especially between the Anglican churches of the United Kingdom and the Lutheran churches of Northern Europe, there have been lively discussions about the renewal of the diaconate and its place in or relation to the Church's ordained ministry. The diaconate was a major topic in the consultations which resulted in the Porvoo Communion. Early on in the Porvoo conversations, the churches committed to working toward a common understanding of diaconal ministry and have held several consultations on the diaconate and diaconal ministry.

Norway

While the Church of Norway agrees that diaconal work is part of the nature of the Church and an important component of the ministry of every congregation, for several decades the language was intentionally ambiguous about the ordination of deacons. The documents leave open the possibility that deacons are part of the Church's ordained ministry as well as the possibility of deacons being a lay ministry. The Church strongly encouraged employment of deacons, especially in larger parishes and every diocese, and the National Council was required to have a diaconal adviser. In addition, it was deemed appropriate for deacons to be engaged by a variety of diaconal institutions and agencies with formal and informal connections with the Church of Norway. Even the liturgical rite authorizing deacons leaves open some ambiguity.

The *Plan for Diakonia* indicates that the presence of a deacon in a parish is important in implementing the Church's diaconal tasks, which are identified as:

1. loving your neighbour;
2. creating inclusive communities;
3. caring for creation;
4. working for justice.

The role of the parish deacon sometimes is to provide direct care, for example, counselling, advocating, and ministering to the ill and homebound. The deacon also plans, coordinates, directs, trains, etc., for effective *diakonia* by the members of the congregation. The deacon may also serve in a liturgical function, especially in the "high mass". For these tasks, deacons are educated both theologically and professionally.

At the same time, there remain several communities—sisterhoods and brotherhoods—which are associated with the historical centres of diaconal work. Both men and women may belong to these communities or orders. In some of the communities some members have also been "ordained" deacons and some are ordained as pastors/priests.

Sweden

Unlike most other Lutheran churches, the Church of Sweden ordained deacons for about a hundred years after the Protestant Reformation. For some, the diaconate was a transitional state on the way to being ordained priests. Some, however, remained deacons, often assisting the bishop or priest. Their work was not primarily charitable in nature but was seen as a liturgical–pastoral order. In the hierarchy of ministry, deacon was considered inferior to bishop and priest. In the mid-seventeenth century, the Church of Sweden stopped ordaining deacons.

In the nineteenth century, there was a revival of *diakonia* in Sweden, following the German model. From the middle of the nineteenth century to the middle of the twentieth century, there was discussion of other approaches to the diaconate that would not be communal and would be more integrated into the Church's ministry. The Church of Sweden also developed an understanding of *diakonia* as a core part of the Church's being and one of its essential functions. There was a desire to see the diaconal life of the Church more closely connected to its liturgy. By 1942, the diaconate was seen as an office of the Church and by 1987 the diaconate was acknowledged as part of the threefold ordained ministry—bishop, priest, deacon. Members of the deaconess and deacon communities could choose to become part of the ordained diaconate. Some did and some did not.

Since 1999, the office of deacon has been formally regulated in the ordinances of the Church of Sweden. Deacons assume various roles in the life of the congregations where they serve, depending on local needs. They may be teachers, administrators, youth ministers, counsellors, home visitors. They are most often involved in care of the elderly, work among children and candidates for confirmation, group and individual counselling, work with families, refugee work. They may also be involved in social work among people with addictions and those on the margins of society. Deacons are also involved liturgically in assisting at the mass—reading the gospel, leading the prayers, and serving the chalice.

Finland

The Evangelical Lutheran Church of Finland (ELCF) was also influenced by the German developments of diaconal communities. After a time, some deacons and other church leaders began to question this model and suggested that diaconal work would be more appropriately located in the parishes. The proposal gained support, and in 1943 or 1944 the Church decided that each parish would be required to create a post for one or more deacons/deaconesses. (In Finland, the difference between deacon and deaconess is not related to gender but rather to their education and function. Deaconesses—mostly women—are trained as nurses and may work in hospitals or parishes. Deacons—both women and men—are trained in social work and may serve in parishes or social service organizations in the community.)

With the decision in the 1940s came a period of renewal and redevelopment of the diaconate in the Church. It also meant that the diaconate was now legally connected to the Church and functioned within the Church's ministry. Deacons and deaconesses were set apart for this ministry by a bishop with laying-on of hands and prayers for the gift of the Holy Spirit. Deacons/deaconesses in the ELCF are not given specific liturgical roles. They may assist with the distribution of Communion, but any member of the parish may do so at the invitation of the pastor. The tasks of the deacon/deaconess are outlined as follows:

1. To develop diaconal work as part of holistic parish work, to identify where service is needed and the reasons which lie behind needs, and to seek ways in which the parish can help people in need;
2. To give direct help to those in need, to identify people's needs and to provide care for clients in their own homes and at the deacon's office during office hours;
3. To encourage parish members to take responsibility for others and for the environment and to lead them in the action which needs to be taken;
4. To train and support people (including diaconal lay personnel) in different tasks in diaconal parish work;
5. To disseminate information about diaconal work on different levels in the church;
6. To provide information on diaconal work inside and outside the parish;
7. To cooperate, in the vocational and voluntary field, with public social work and health care personnel;
8. To work on the parish board of diaconal work, to take the minutes of the board, make operational plans, and draw up annual budgets and reports of diaconal work undertaken.

Increasingly, diaconal work has moved from healthcare toward pastoral care and focus on economic conditions and reacting to legislation and social practices. It has also been extended to international concern for human rights and economic aid. It is clear that the diaconate is moving into a more prophetic role in the Church and society.

Estonia

The Estonian Evangelical Lutheran Church established the office of deacon as a permanent order in the early 1990s. Deacons are one of three orders (also including bishops and priests) of the one ordained ministry. The Church's constitution describes deacons as assistants to priests, and most of them serve in small congregations that have no resident priest. The documents of the Church primarily describe their liturgical functions, which can include administering the sacraments.

Denmark

In the Lutheran Church of Denmark there have been deaconess motherhouses and institutions after the Kaiserswerth model since the Royal Family helped initiate them in the mid-1860s. In addition to serving in institutions, deaconesses served in parishes throughout Denmark. The Lutheran Church of Denmark did not sign the Porvoo agreement until 2010 and has been a latecomer to the related conversations about the renewal of the diaconate.

Iceland

The Evangelical Lutheran Church of Iceland formally established an ordained diaconate as a result of its involvement in the Porvoo Communion. It formerly had a few deacons and deaconesses, but there were no official rules established by the Church for them. The Church established standards of preparation and opened a programme for training deacons in 1993 at Reykjavik University. The rite of ordination is used for both parish deacons and diocesan deacons.

Lithuania

The Evangelical Lutheran Church of Lithuania ordains bishops, pastors and deacons. Because of a shortage of pastors after the Second World War and to comply with laws of the Soviet Union, the Church ordained pastor–deacons to serve in parishes when no trained and ordained pastors were available. About thirty years ago, the Church began to study a more traditional diaconate and has begun to ordain deacons as part of a threefold ministry.

Lutheran diaconates in the Southern Hemisphere

The Evangelical Church of the Lutheran Confession in Brazil (IECLB)

Since 1992, the IECLB has ordained diaconal ministers—women and men. The roots of this ministry are traced to the beginning of the twentieth century, when deacons and deaconesses came from Germany to serve the immigrants who had begun coming from Germany in 1824. Eventually, because of a shortage of pastors, all the male deacons were ordained pastors. In 1939, a deaconess motherhouse was founded at São Leopoldo following the Kaiserswerth model.

Influenced by liberation theology, the leaders of the IECLB came to understand that the Church's mission was not just to their own people but for the sake of the world. They found that *diakonia* was the term that captured their broader understanding of mission and ministry. The IECLB adopted a statement *Shared Ministry* in 1992, taking seriously the LWF's encouragement to shape public ministry in ways appropriate to their context. The diaconate became one of four equal expressions of ordained ministries within the IECLB—pastors, diaconal ministers, catechists and evangelists. Members of the deaconess community were included as diaconal ministers. (The Portuguese is *obeiros* (male) or *obeiras* (female) for all ordained ministers; *diaconais* designates them as diaconal.) People in all four tracks of ordained ministry receive the same basic seminary education. Students in each of the areas also receive courses in their own specialty. They have equal voting rights within the Church, and they all serve with the same salary scale. The specific responsibilities of the diaconal ministry are to:

- Stimulate acts of love and service to people in need;
- Promote diaconal spirituality among members;
- Form groups of solidarity or service in the congregation;
- Carry out diaconal activities in institutions such as hospitals, homes for children or the elderly and others;
- Participate in ecumenical activities that aim to protect human dignity and justice, supported by the congregation;

- Uphold congregational initiatives that aim to prevent or heal human suffering and remove its causes;
- Cooperate in the implementation of social projects.

Diaconal ministers also participate in preaching and leading worship, wearing an alb and deacon stole.

Indonesia

Beginning in 1891, deaconesses from Kaiserswerth, Germany, came to work among the Batak people. They trained women in nursing and other professions and organized a motherhouse according to the German tradition. This was the foundation of the diaconate in the HKBP (*Huria Kristen Batak Protestant*). Although the motherhouse was not structurally part of the Church, the deaconesses were eventually consecrated by the Church and recognized as well prepared for ministry.

After World War II and the exodus of the German missionaries, the HKBP developed a more indigenous approach to its diaconal work and established a sisterhood at Balige in 1961. This community thrives today. By 1983, deaconesses were ordained and received the same rights and roles as pastors, teacher–preachers and *biblevrow* (Bible women). Today, deaconesses provide leadership for the Church's ministries of health, social service and advocacy.

Kenya

The Evangelical Lutheran Church in Kenya has for the past twenty years educated and consecrated deaconesses to work especially with women, children and the sick, primarily in parishes.

Tanzania

The Evangelical Lutheran Church in Tanzania has at least two diocesan-based communities of deaconesses established by deaconess motherhouses from Germany. The sisters live a common life and serve in schools, health ministries and other agencies of the Church. At least one other diocese has begun a parish-based diaconate of women.

India

The Tamil Evangelical Lutheran Church in India has a community of deaconesses after the German motherhouse model.

North America

Lutheranism in North America has been influenced by its roots in Europe. Immigrants from Germany and the Scandinavian countries brought their language, theology, liturgy and practices of public ministry. That influence can be seen throughout both the United States and Canada. It was the powerful witness of the German deaconesses that sparked clergymen and businessmen alike to bring deaconesses to North America to set up motherhouses, organize and staff hospitals, and begin institutions to care for those in need and schools for children and youth. When deaconesses were first brought to this continent, they largely followed the Kaiserswerth model. In this, there was little church connection; the motherhouses were governed by boards of men, and clergymen were often involved in the day-to-day operation. By the late 1800s there were upwards of one hundred Lutheran deaconess communities, usually connected with hospitals or other institutions. Only some lasted for more than a few years.

Even when a diaconate went out of existence, the institution they had founded may continue and thrive to this day. The following stories illustrate some of that history:

> Pastor Wm Passavant, in 1849 brought deaconesses to Pittsburgh to found a motherhouse and a hospital. While the community has not continued, Passavant Hospital offers excellent healthcare today. Pastor E. A. Fogelstrom founded Immanuel Hospital in Omaha, with a deaconess community using a floor of the hospital as its motherhouse. This hospital recognizes its reliance on deaconesses, although the last deaconess from that community has retired. The Lutheran Medical Center in Brooklyn is the result of a Norwegian deaconess, whose brother-in-law requested her help to minister to Norwegian seamen. Each year, staff

and patients hear the story of Sister Elizabeth Fedde, and she "walks" the halls in her garb, telling the story of how it all began. A businessman, John Lankenau, was president of the Lutheran Hospital in Philadelphia (now named Lankenau Hospital) and arranged for deaconesses to come from Iserlohn, Germany, to restructure and staff the hospital. He wanted deaconesses to turn it into a healthy and life-giving place; they did. They also added parish work, a school for girls and a kindergarten. And there were others, in Chicago, Milwaukee, Minneapolis, St Paul, Brush, Bethphage, and more. Some connected with Norwegian Lutherans, others with German or Swedish.

A second historical strand is that of the Church instituting a diaconate. The General Synod of the Lutheran Church opened a motherhouse in Baltimore in 1895. It created a Board of Deaconess Work and designated deaconesses as an "office of the Church", thus committing the Church to promote and support the deaconess community.

The roots of these early communities continue in two communities still thriving today.

Deaconess Community of the Evangelical Lutheran Church in America

The Deaconess Community of the Evangelical Lutheran Church in America (ELCA) came from the joining of three communities, Baltimore, Philadelphia and Omaha, at the time the Lutheran Church in America (LCA) came into being in 1962 through a merger with several Lutheran church bodies. The relationship between Church and Community was complex. The LCA oversaw the Community by electing the board that governed the Community. An Executive Director for the Community was employed by the Church. The Baltimore Community sold its buildings and the motherhouse was situated in Gladwyne, Philadelphia. When the LCA joined with two other church bodies to become the ELCA in 1988, the Deaconess Community entered into a formal relationship with the ELCA. The Community continued to elect its own Directing Deaconess and formulate its own policies; these policies needed to be approved by the Church. In 2002, the Community sold the Gladwyne house and moved its headquarters to Chicago. This Community is still active and part of the ELCA, also serving the Evangelical Lutheran Church in Canada (ELCIC).

The Community now comprises about seventy-five deaconesses, serving as teachers, counsellors, administrators, health professionals, Christian educators, youth workers, information specialists, ecumenists, and more, in congregations, synod offices, hospitals, social service agencies, outdoor ministries and universities. As part of the official rostered ministry, they provide leadership in the formation, education and empowerment of all the baptized in the ministry of *diakonia*.

Lutheran Diaconal Association

The Lutheran Diaconal Association (LDA) [formerly Lutheran Deaconess Association] was founded in 1919 in Fort Wayne, Indiana, also on the German motherhouse model. By 1943, the motherhouse was abandoned. The education moved to Valparaiso University and the LDA offices were relocated to Valparaiso. The locus of ministry moved from hospitals and institutions to parishes and agencies.

The LDA has remained free-standing and inter-Lutheran. Some of its 400+ deaconesses and deacons serve in ministries associated with the ELCA, ELCIC, Lutheran Church–Missouri Synod, and several other Lutheran church bodies. Others serve in settings outside church bodies and maintain connections with the communities of deaconesses and deacons.

Today the LDA has an education/formation process that is based in four areas of competency: Theology, Spirituality, Work/Ministry, and Community. It includes developing and honing skills, attitudes and values related to *diakonia* through academic study, hands-on practice, student seminars, and mentoring by members of the community. The call to diaconal ministry is lived out in a variety of professions and occupations. LDA deaconesses and deacons serve as nurses, parish ministers, chaplains, attorneys, educators, social workers, spiritual directors, church musicians, therapists, administrators, and more. Some are also found on the rosters of the church bodies in which they serve as deaconesses, deacons or pastors.

Evangelical Lutheran Church in Canada (ELCIC)

The ELCIC came into being in 1986. At the time of merger, no decision had been reached about the diaconate. Prior to merger, an agreement had been reached that the Deaconess Community would be able to serve in Canada, as it had been doing since the 1940s. Two years after merger, a task force was formed to study what the formation of public ministry should be. The study took five years and used the WCC's *Baptism, Eucharist and Ministry* document, the LWF statements, Lutheran theology and biblical information to create its recommendation: one ordination and three forms (bishop, presbyter, deacon). Instead, at its National Convention a simple motion was passed that this new church would have "bishops, pastors and diaconal ministers", with further study of entrance rites to be undertaken.

In 1995, a motion was passed that all deaconesses working within this church would be grand-parented onto the roster. Thus an ELCIC diaconate was formed which included members of the Deaconess Community of the ELCA and of the LDA. Course requirements were developed and constitution and by-laws were appropriately changed. The entrance rite was consecration and diaconal ministers were categorized as "lay". Recently the word "lay" was removed from the constitution, wisdom indicating that being "lay" and "rostered" was an oxymoron. A further ongoing study will likely recommend that deacons be ordained. Deacons serve as pastors in congregations where there is no pastor available, as chaplains in social service institutions, such as nursing homes, in congregations as youth, education and music ministers, and in synodical and national offices. There are around thirty deacons, about half of whom are retired.

The Standards for Ordained Ministry and for Diaconal Ministry begin with the same definition: someone who:

- is rooted in the gospel;
- is knowledgeable, passionate, able to articulate his or her faith and the confessional teachings of the ELCIC; and
- through the Church participates in God's mission of love, redemption, justice and reconciliation.

Diaconal ministry candidates are to demonstrate competencies in these areas: spiritual and personal formation, vocational awareness, diaconal identity, adherence to Lutheran theology, missional awareness, cultural context, capacity for public ministerial leadership. Except for "diaconal identity", these competencies are identical to those required for ordained ministry, which translates identity into "pastoral identity".

The Evangelical Lutheran Church in America (ELCA)

Each of the three church bodies which came together in 1988 to form the ELCA had lay ministries, including parish workers, lay professional leaders, deaconesses and teachers. In typical Lutheran fashion, a task force was established to study how these ministries would be recognized in the new Church and what sort of "lay" ministries the ELCA would have going forward.

The task force's deliberations, as in the ELCIC, were influenced by the WCC's *Baptism, Eucharist and Ministry*, by conversations with ecumenical and global partners, and by theological and historical study. In 1993, the ELCA established three "lay" rosters: Deaconesses (members of the Deaconess Community of the ELCA), Associates in Ministry (including most of the lay ministers from the predecessor church bodies and new candidates who would serve primarily within parishes), and Diaconal Ministers. It was the hope that Diaconal Ministers would lead the church in *diakonia* and serve as a connection between church and world. While the matter of entrance rite was hotly discussed and debated, the decision was made to "consecrate", not "ordain" Diaconal Ministers and Deaconesses. Associates in Ministry were "commissioned".

With the results of a couple of decades of experience, new ecumenical partnerships and the emerging challenges for the Church in today's world, the ELCA acted in 2016 to unify the three "lay" rosters into one roster of "Ministers of Word and Service". The word "lay" was eliminated from the governing documents, which outline two parallel rosters: Ministry of Word and Sacrament (pastors) and Ministry of Word and Service (deacons). The 2019 ELCA Churchwide Assembly will consider the recommendation that deacons be ordained.

These decisions are seen not merely as changes in listings and nomenclature, but as changes that will help the whole Church better live out its calling to *diakonia* and be poised for more relevant witness in the world. This intention is expressed in the list of responsibilities in the ELCA's constitution.

> (E)very minister of Word and Service shall:
>
> a. be rooted in the Word of God, for proclamation and service;
> b. advocate a prophetic diakonia that commits itself to risk-taking and innovative service on the frontiers of the Church's outreach, giving particular attention to the suffering places in God's world;
> c. speak publicly to the world in solidarity with the poor and oppressed, calling for justice and proclaiming God's love for the world, witnessing to the realm of God in the community, the nation and abroad;
> d. equip the baptized for ministry in God's world that affirms the gifts of all people;
> e. encourage mutual relationships that invite participation and accompaniment of others in God's mission;
> f. practice stewardship that respects God's gift of time, talents and resources;
> g. be grounded in a gathered community for ongoing diaconal formation;
> h. share knowledge of the ELCA and its wider ministry of the gospel and advocate for the work of all expressions of this church; and
> i. identify and encourage qualified persons to prepare for ministry of the gospel.

Currently, there are approximately 1,600 deacons in the ELCA. About half of them are retired or on-leave-from-call. Their roles include parish and agency administrator, church musician, community organizer, synod and church-wide staff, social worker, teacher, youth and family minister, college president, volunteer coordinator, faith formation director, spiritual director, therapist, chaplain, and more. Deacons do not have a prescribed role in liturgy but often serve as leaders and preachers when congregations gather for worship.

Concluding comments

Diaconates have taken many shapes and forms within Lutheran churches. There is a rich history. Despite the many challenges, or perhaps because of them, diaconates continue to strive to be true to the call from God, *diakonia*. This expression of ministry is especially needed in North America today, as the Church seeks to re-imagine its future. The women and men of these Lutheran diaconates demonstrate collaborative leadership, ecumenical commitments, and a spirituality that focuses on being the incarnation of the servant Christ wherever there is need. While the churches have been largely pastor-centric, the diaconate models a ministry that holds companionship and empowerment as key values. The diaconate as it expresses its prophetic nature can help the Church realize its mission for the sake of the world today. Thanks be to God.

CHAPTER 11

The Diaconate as Ecumenical Opportunity

Maylanne Maybee

When I speak about the ecumenical opportunities presented by the diaconate, I want to start with ecumenical in the broadest sense—*oikumene*, meaning the whole inhabited earth! We are not just talking about interdenominational understanding, but about a perspective that embraces religion, thought and politics and recognizes every human pursuit as subject to the healing ministry of Christ's Spirit. Within that perspective, we are considering what *diakonia* might be in its broadest sense. I believe we are talking about God's longing for all who inhabit the earth to live in *shalom*, in harmony with one another and creation. I like to borrow the Hebrew term, *tikkun olam*, to talk about our human responsibility for fixing what is wrong with the world.

God's mission incarnated in Jesus demonstrated the depth and breadth of that longing and the human cost of that fixing. A mark of God's mission is that it was directed to the least among us. So for me, *diakonia* takes on the meaning of mission and ministry and also the way in which Jesus lived out that ministry, the way he challenged the principalities and powers of this world, and the way he responded with compassion and healing to the *anawim*, the "little ones", who are so often excluded or oppressed by the systems that are created and maintained by those principalities and powers.

Personal introduction

In some ways, I feel uniquely qualified to speak about ecumenical opportunities with regard to the diaconate in the narrower and more focused sense. My own vocational journey as a deacon has been very ecumenical. After graduating with my first degree in Toronto, I spent two years in Oxford, where I lived in the house of St Gregory and St Macrina, operated by the Orthodox Chaplaincy. My rooms were directly above the chapel, and on my first morning there, a Sunday, I was awakened by the deep voice of the deacon singing the Prayer of the Faithful in Old Slavonic. I sang in the choir for the Divine Liturgy for the two years I lived there and experienced week by week the liturgical presence of a deacon.

Upon my return to Canada in the early 1970s, I wrestled with a sense of call just at the time that women were being considered for ordination to the priesthood in the Episcopal Church and in the Anglican Church of Canada. For various reasons I did not feel drawn to parish ministry and was much more interested in the Church's mission "in the world", especially in local neighbourhoods. At this point, I was introduced to the movement to restore the diaconate as a ministry and order with its own integrity and immediately felt at home.

Since then, I have experienced many ecumenical expressions and explorations of the diaconate. In 1995, I participated in an Anglican–Lutheran consultation on the diaconate and a special meeting of the Anglican–Lutheran International Commission, resulting in *The Hanover Report*, "The Diaconate as Ecumenical Opportunity". It was the first time I witnessed the deep respect, openness and attentiveness that characterized the conversations between those two churches. In the 1990s, I participated as an observer in the Working Party of the House of Bishops of the Church of England that produced the 2001 study *At such a time as this—a renewed diaconate in the Church of England.*

While on a sabbatical leave in 2003, I visited Taizé, where I met a Roman Catholic deacon from the Diocese of Meaux (which includes Charles de Gaulle Airport in its boundaries). He had a special commission from his bishop for youth ministry and was taking a group of young people from his diocese on a pilgrimage. His day job was cleaning graffiti for the city of Paris. He and his family hosted me for a weekend at their home in Meaux, where he introduced me to the team of clergy of the diocese. Besides attending to young people, he also did a lot of marriage preparation and presiding at weddings—telling couples not to call him "Father", as the only people who did so were his two children! It was an encounter that gave me a vision of what the diaconate could be, especially if embraced, supported and used by the diocesan bishop.

For six years, I served as principal at the Centre for Christian Studies, based in Winnipeg, a small theological college that represents the coming-together of Anglican and United Church training schools for women. As principal, I was embraced by the diaconal community of the United Church of Canada, a body that is both wide and deep and rich in the diaconal tradition.

And so, my life as a deacon has given me insights from the Orthodox tradition, the Anglican Communion, from Lutheranism, and the Reformed tradition of the United Church of Canada. I have also had the chance to participate in ecumenical associations, including two assemblies of the World Diakonia and several gatherings of the Diakonia of the Americas and the Caribbean. And I have been recruited to the Anglican–Roman Catholic Dialogue of Canada.

Context

In 1982, while researching for my MDiv thesis on "The Diaconate: A Ministry of Servanthood and Leadership" and in the years after, when I was seeking to deepen my understanding of this office, I found a wealth of emerging material to draw from:

1. The 1979 *Book of Common Prayer* of the Episcopal Church was foundational in my thinking about ministry. The biggest innovation in the American Prayer Book revision was to re-establish the primacy and centrality of baptism as the key rite of initiation into the Christian life. The idea of baptism as full initiation into the body of Christ was for me the beginning of a redefinition of my understanding of church, of ministry and of ordination.

2. Bishop Wes Frensdorff, Episcopal Bishop of Nevada, at this time began to give life to a new vision of baptism and ministry which became known as Total Ministry, based on the recognition that the Holy Spirit is active in local communities of the faithful and not defined by theological degrees or restricted to the hierarchical structures of the Church. He spoke of the orders as "offices" within the life and mission of the Church that give sacramental focus to the corporate ministry of the baptized.

3. The World Council of Churches document, *Baptism, Eucharist and Ministry (BEM)*, published in 1982, inspired me with its clear and very positive overview of the concept of a threefold ministry as grounds for ecumenical understanding.

4. Another key source was Edward Schillebeeckx's book, *Ministry: Leadership in the Community of Jesus Christ*, published in 1981. Schillebeeckx was one of the most active theologians at the Second Vatican Council and exercised an important influence on the document *Lumen gentium*, a doctrinal restatement of the nature of the Church, which shifted emphasis from a fixed and hierarchical view of church and ministry to one that envisioned a more balanced and collegial exercise of authority. *Lumen gentium* also endorsed the revival of the office of deacon as found in the early Church as a permanent vocation.

Together, these documents represent a deep ecumenical awakening that was happening at the time—the 1979 *Book of Common Prayer*, the Canons for Total Ministry, *BEM* or *Baptism, Eucharist and Ministry*, *Lumen gentium*. I confess that I expected a more visible and lively renewal of the Church and its ministry, but it has unfolded at a much slower pace than I anticipated.

Diakonia and the diaconate

How do the Anglican Church of Canada and the Episcopal Church understand the diaconate? The service of ordination for deacons in the 1979 Episcopal *Book of Common Prayer* (BCP) is similar to the one in the 1985 *Book of Alternative Services* (BAS) of the Anglican Church of Canada, but not identical. I often point out these distinguishing features in the service of ordination for a deacon as compared to that of a priest or presbyter:

- *Deacons* are called to a special ministry of servanthood, directly under the authority of the bishop. *Priests* are called to work as pastor, priest and teacher, together with the bishop and fellow presbyters, and to take their share in the councils of the Church.
- *Deacons* are to serve all people, especially the poor, the weak, the sick and the lonely. *Presbyters* are to care alike for young and old, strong and weak, rich and poor.
- *Deacons* are to interpret to the Church the needs, concerns, and hopes of the world. *Presbyters* are to preach, declare God's forgiveness and pronounce God's blessing.
- *Deacons* are to assist the bishop and presybters in administering God's word and sacraments, and to carry out other duties as assigned. *Presbyters* are to preside at baptism, Eucharist, and other ministrations entrusted to them.

Clearly, the emphasis is on the "servanthood" aspect of the diaconate and its role of serving the poor and the helpless. This was a reflection of the meaning that scholars commonly ascribed to the Greek word *diakonia*, most often translated within the New Testament as "ministry" or "humble or lowly service".

But the work of John N. Collins, which did not appear until 1990, has challenged this consensus. His study of *diakonia* and its cognates concluded that the word is better understood to mean "the carrying out of a commissioned task" rather than the more traditional "humble service". By extension, his re-interpretation emphasizes the functions of a *diakonos* as being a messenger or go-between, an agent or ambassador, an attendant to a household or an important person charged with a particular task or responsibility. *The Hanover Report* strives for a compromise by summing up diaconal ministers as "those who are called to be agents of the Church in interpreting and meeting needs, hopes, and concerns within church and society".

When I talk about the ministry of deacons, I prefer to stay with the Greek word *diakonia* because I do not think we have settled yet on a definitive English translation. I love Ormonde Plater's popularization of the folk etymology of *diakonia* as "through the dust". It conveys the idea of a fast-moving messenger, a courier, someone who urgently carries important news from one person to another. He also compared the role of deacons to that of angelic messengers, such as Gabriel visiting Mary of Nazareth, or the angels who ministered to Jesus in the wilderness.

The stance taken by *Baptism, Eucharist and Ministry* confirmed the need for a more credible expression of the diaconate by more clearly linking the diaconal role of service to the world with liturgical functions. In 2002, Deaconess Louise Williams of the Lutheran Deaconess Community in the United States gave a keynote address in Winnipeg to a gathering of the Diakonia of the Americas and the Caribbean on five images of *diakonia*, based on an article by Antonia Linn that did just that. I offer these as a useful way to highlight the common understanding we share in our traditions of the role of deacons.

These five images are: servant, table waiter, story-teller, go-between, and guardian of the light. They relate to the diaconal actions from scripture and liturgy of washing feet, preparing the eucharistic table, performing the ablutions, proclaiming the Gospel, standing metaphorically at the door to welcome and send forth the faithful, and bearing the Paschal Candle at the Easter Vigil, when the deacon joyfully sings the *Exsultet*, announcing Jesus' resurrection from the dead. I believe these images combine the traditional notion of service with Collins' redefinition of the deacon as agent, go-between and attendant. While they do not define *diakonia*, they give it contour and meaning. Whereas the priest assembles people, gathers them at the table, and brings to remembrance Christ's sacrifice through the elements of bread and wine, the deacon recalls the needs and hopes of the world beyond the assembly, models Jesus' self-emptying ministry in carrying out the acts of a servant, and sends the people out in mission.

People often speak of the deacon's ministry as doing or modelling acts of charity and justice. But Roman Catholic deacon William Ditewig has said:

The mistake I see quite often here in the United States is to confuse the deacon's mission with charity alone or even just charity and justice. That's too limiting. I refer to deacons as 'ministers of connect the dots'. We are supposed to show how charity and justice are a function of word and sacrament. They all fit together—they're not separate, distinct compartments.[1]

Yes.

Douglas John Hall was a United Church of Canada theologian who more than anything was a contextual theologian and wrote extensively about how the Church can survive in an era where it is no longer triumphant. He asked the question, "What is the mission of a church that is no longer held in favour in Western civilization and can no longer depend on that status to ensure its meaning and continued existence?"[2] His answer? The Church must begin to witness and serve outside or on the edge of the dominant culture. For the Church to survive and be faithful to its message, it must change or ultimately die. This is the diaconal task of the Church, its sacred mission in twenty-first-century North America, and it needs deacons who are gifted, trained and skilled to fulfil this task.

The meaning of ordination

When writing my thesis, I was particularly interested in the meaning of ordination and why the Church would ordain deacons when they did not have the same clarity of function in ministry and liturgy as presbyters and bishops. More than anything, the 1979 BCP of the Episcopal Church helped to put the sacrament of ordination in perspective by shifting the concept and locus of "character", always so strongly attributed to the priesthood, to baptism. Thus, the means by which I participate in the priesthood of Christ is through baptism. Likewise, the means by which I participate in the *diakonia* or sacred mission of Christ is through baptism. The means by which I join in the *episcope*, the universal life in Christ as it has been handed down, is through baptism. This was creatively and eloquently expressed in the language of the Baptismal Covenant.

The experimentation of Bishop Wes Frensdorff with the model of Total Ministry was also helpful to me. I appreciated his concept of orders as "offices" that give sacramental focus to the priestly, diaconal and episcopal ministry of the baptized. The laying-on of hands is the outward visible sign of the inward spiritual grace of authorized leadership that is both affirmed and recognized by the people of God and is strengthened by the gift of the Holy Spirit. If we choose to understand baptism as the action that confers priestly and diaconal character to the people of God, it helps put into perspective the cherished assumption by many that priests are deacons too. This may be so, but I believe they are "deacons" through baptism, not through an earlier act of ordination. If we were to be consistent, we would also resume the practice of direct ordination (i.e. ordination to the priesthood, or for that matter to the episcopate, without passing through the diaconate first). Though I think it may be desirable and logical, I am not sure it is possible in a church that has not yet embraced the significance and fullness of baptism.

I was inspired by the renewed vision of baptism and ministry based on the recognition that the Holy Spirit is active in local communities of the faithful and not restricted to the hierarchical structures of the Church. Schillebeeckx reminds us that in the early Church the Eucharist could always take place when the community met together. This offers an important corrective to the practice of the so-called "deacon's mass", which involves the distribution and reception of "pre-consecrated" elements, as if their consecration was distinct and separate from the life of the gathered community.

The Hanover Report of the Anglican–Lutheran International Commission describes ordination as both an activity and an identity. It is open-ended and lifelong; it resides within the one ordained ministry of Word and Sacrament; it has a symbolic as well as practical relationship to the whole community. Among Anglicans and Roman Catholics, we share the language and practice of ordination to all three orders within the one sacramental order—appointment by the bishop on behalf of the people of God with prayer and the laying-on of hands. As *BEM* affirms, the key elements of ordination consist in:

- calling by the community;
- appointment to or for a community;
- laying-on of hands by other ministers;
- offering of *epiclesis* by all concerned.

In the United and Lutheran Churches, the understanding of the diaconate has been influenced by the evolution of that ministry from the deaconess movement that came into prominence during the Industrial Revolution of the nineteenth century. It was the means by which women could participate in the Church's leadership with authority and accountability. The ministry that they pioneered continued after women were admitted into the ordained ministry of both those churches. For reasons of culture and identity, diaconal ministers in the United Church are "commissioned" and in the Lutheran Church they are "consecrated"—but always with the marks of ordination as an act of appointment with prayer and the laying-on of hands by others in authorized ministry.

Issues arising from a distinctive diaconate

The Roman Catholic deacon Kenan Osborne, in his 2006 book *The Permanent Diaconate: Its History and Place in the Sacrament of Orders*, reflects on both the gifts and the issues arising from the re-establishment of the permanent diaconate since Vatican II. He discusses theological, pastoral and personal issues, all of which arise from the central question about the precise role of the diaconate within the ordained leadership of the Church today. From my observation, the issues he identified apply equally to the Anglican Church of Canada.

A prevailing concern is the boundary issues regarding the role of deacons vis-à-vis the roles of priest or pastor, bishop and lay leaders:

- Deacons are often not part of many leadership and decision-making bodies that revolve around the presbyterate;
- Their liturgical functions are unclear or inconsistent, such as preaching, baptizing, officiating at weddings or funerals, anointing the sick;

- Many tasks of deacons can also be done by lay ministers; and
- Pastorally, there is the question of who does what? i.e. specific roles and tasks tend to flounder without theological clarity.

Theologically, Osborne asks how deacons fit into the one Sacred Order, alongside bishops and presbyters. "It is the foundational interrelationship of bishop, priest, and deacon in the one sacrament of order that is theologically unclear."[3] At the personal level, the re-establishment of the diaconate raises the matter of diaconal self-identity. Without clarity, a morale problem can arise—are deacons appreciated for what they have been asked to do? For the time and energy they expend on their ministry, often without financial remuneration?

Ecumenical opportunity

The notion of "Receptive Ecumenism" seeks to make ecumenical progress by learning from our partners through self-examination and an inner conversion that comes from openness to being transformed by God's grace. I believe Anglicans and other traditions have much to learn from Roman Catholic experience and practice. In particular:

- Their clear sense of continuity with and faithfulness to the apostolic origins of the Church. Recent scholarship has given us considerable detail and insight into these origins, which are not so obvious and incontrovertible as we might have once thought. Our mutual task then is to attend to the nuances of our shared and separate histories with regard to the diaconate, to discern what to recover, what to let go of, and what to adapt creatively to our context.
- Their formal processes of decision-making and authority. While Vatican II initiated the re-establishment of the permanent diaconate as a major part of the sacrament of orders, implementation was left to local episcopal conferences. Not all such conferences took action, but enough to give the diaconate a robust presence in the Church's official ministry and to make it a substantial theme in

the renewal of clerical leadership in the Roman Catholic Church of today. It appears that these formal processes have given *gravitas* to the decision and momentum to enacting it.

- Their high standards of formation for the diaconate, which appear to be more consistent and rigorous than in many parts of the Anglican Church of Canada. Though contextual factors are important, I wonder whether practices that vary so greatly are what make it so difficult to know what the glue is that holds the diaconal order together.

- Their emphasis on a stable personal life and on the balance of family life and ministry, marked by the practice of including the spouses of diaconal candidates in training and formation and even requiring their participation.

I also think Anglicans have things to share:

- Our experience of women who served as deaconesses or deacons, because they did not have other options for authorized ministry. In many ways, they breathed life and vitality into the diaconate and themselves became enriched by their time in that order. We have much to learn from the creativity, resourcefulness, flexibility and pioneering spirit of these women who went on to assume other forms of leadership.

- On the other hand, there is our experience of women and men in the diaconate because they want to be and feel called to be there. At times, the diaconate functioned as a kind of holding place for women who really felt called to the priesthood, but now that that option has been opened to them the diaconate has been able to claim its own distinctiveness and integrity.

- What we have learned from Total Ministry or Local Collaborative Ministry, a model that takes seriously the presence and activity of the Holy Spirit in local communities while heeding the importance of the catholicity and universality of orders.

Finally, let me borrow good ideas from *The Hanover Report* for enjoying the ecumenical opportunity presented by a renewed diaconate:

- Sharing the ministry of deacons and diaconal ministers of either tradition, borrowing or seconding deacons in areas where one or the other tradition is sparsely represented;
- Joint presentations at synodical or convention gatherings on the "needs, hopes and concerns of the world" as perceived and experienced by deacons;
- Invitations to deacons of one tradition to participate in the liturgies of the other, particularly on major occasions;
- Opening up diaconal associations to membership from both traditions;
- Initiating demonstration projects using pooled resources to encourage experimentation and learning with regard to:
  - new patterns of stipendiary and non-stipendiary ministry;
  - theological and ministerial training and formation;
  - encouraging and supporting churches which may not at this time have a diaconate to initiate a diaconate as appropriate to their ministry needs.

One of the things I appreciate about the principle of Receptive Ecumenism is the awareness that there is a spiritual process whereby the decisions of council or formal bodies of the Church become part of the life of the local church—and vice versa. There is opportunity to learn from each other what we have experienced in the course of that spiritual process.

And, as articulated in *BEM*, Receptive Ecumenism gives us the chance to learn and benefit from the richness of the whole *oikumene*, to help each other focus on our identity in a way that helps us learn, grow and change and to become true to our apostolic origins. May it be so.

Notes

[1] "A Call of Their Own: The Role of Deacons in the Church", an interview with Deacon William Ditewig, an article that appeared in the June 2014 issue of *U.S. Catholic* (79:6, pp. 24–28). <https://www.uscatholic.org/articles/201406/call-their-own-role-deacons-church-28973>.

[2]   Douglas John Hall, "Cross and Context: How My Mind Has Changed", *The Christian Century*, 26 August 2010. <https://www.christiancentury.org/article/2010-08/cross-and-context>.

[3]   Kenan B. Osborne, OFM, *The Permanent Diaconate: Its History and Place in the Sacrament of Orders* (New York/Mahwah, NJ: Paulist Press, 2007), p. 98.

PART 5

The Prophetic Ministry of the Deacon

CHAPTER 12

The Prophetic Role of the Deacon in the Context of Church and Creation

Josephine Borgeson

I recently read a post by a Facebook friend about North Atlantic right whales. No new-born calves have been spotted this year, a cause for ever further alarm about this endangered species. Right whales are baleen whales, feeding near the surface by straining plankton from the ocean water. Because they spend more time this way, and often where other creatures are feeding on the same food source, they are prone to accidents with boats, and worse, entangling in fishers' lines and other equipment. Perhaps it is a relief to think that the main cause of the right whale's demise is not climate change, but fossil fuels do play their part. Lines now are made of plastics, not the plant fibre of old, and are much stronger and break-resistant, leaving the rights often to remain entangled for months and more, with ropes and lines inhibiting their feeding. Skinny whales do not conceive; hence the declining numbers of a species whose numbers are already low.[1]

Normally I don't get overly emotional about poster species, but as someone who liked the cetology material in *Moby Dick*—indeed thought it the most interesting part of the book—my friend's post had me. Then someone posted a comment to the effect that if we don't care even about Black Lives Matter, how can we be bothered with whales? Now I was really engaged. If we don't put our concerns for other people in the context of creation, how can we begin to care at all? I thought.

In the introduction to *Biblical Prophecy: Perspectives for Christian Theology, Discipleship, and Ministry*, Ellen F. Davis lays out five "interrelated and overlapping" elements of the prophetic perspective. What are the elements that might speak to the Church in our place and time? She begins with the idea that prophets must speak of the world as it really is, because without that clear articulation it is impossible to begin to convince people that God is about to do a new thing. I quote in full the second of her five points, where I think she and the biblical prophets she interprets may present the most challenge to our way of constructing our lives today:

> *The prophetic demand for moral, economic, and religious integrity in human communities (Israel or the Church) and recognition that human integrity in these several dimensions is fundamentally related to the God-given integrity of creation.* [Italics hers]

She goes on:

> In the coherent universe evoked by the prophetic traditions, connections are assumed or specifically drawn among phenomena that modernity has generally treated as discrete and unrelated. . .
>
> The prophetic perspective, which perceives these various spheres of our experience as interlocking and interacting, is probably more challenging for interpreters in the modern (or postmodern) period than at any earlier time in history. This is because accepting the prophetic witness as relevant for ourselves means that we must consciously reintegrate aspects of our lives that are habitually separated by the cultural and economic system in which virtually all of us are immersed, which most of us have come to think of as "reality".[2]

Davis develops the idea further, naming this present view of reality as "consumerism", which depends on our ignorance of our connectedness with other creatures and on our fragmentation within ourselves.

I do not think we can speak of the Church as having a prophetic voice in our time, unless it embraces the big picture, a systems view of reality, if you will, an understanding that we, along with countless others, are members of God's creation. When we speak to the details of this time and our several places, we must speak in a way that respects the underlying and permeating connectedness of all creatures.

Of course, there is another dimension to this prophetic work of the Church, the dimension of time. In another "bible", Robert K. Greenleaf's *Servant Leadership*, he spoke of "Foresight—The Central Ethic of Leadership". No mention of the "p" word in Greenleaf, and yet what he identifies as foresight, whilst not the best synonym for prophecy in the biblical sense, seems very akin to it to me. The idea is that instead of thinking of "now" in clock-term times, we think of it as a narrowly-focused beam: "There is a bright intense center, this moment of clock time, and a diminishing intensity . . . on either side."[3] The ability to see the present moment in the context of the past and the probable future is a key quality of leadership. The Church, with our deep awareness of history and tradition in an ahistorical time—when "traditional" is what we did last year—is poised to lead in helping our communities see the present moment more clearly and in context, a gift at the heart of our prophetic calling.

I began talking about the Church, because for a long time I have resisted phrases about the prophetic voice or prophetic ministry of the deacon. I have been most resistant, as you might have guessed, when such descriptions or epithets are used in the singular. I am not completely clear where this resistance in myself comes from, but I think and hope it may be a certain modesty, that no one can claim for herself the role or title of prophet, because prophets are recognized by others, and often too late or even later than that.

How then does the deacon exercise some leadership in the Church's prophetic activity? Decades ago a professor of theology at one of our Episcopal seminaries introduced me to *The Dark Interval* by John Dominic Crossan and to a major theme therein, the contrast between two opposite kinds of story, myth and parable. *Myth* is a story that reconciles the apparently irreconcilable. Myth encourages us to believe in the possibility of a solution. *Parable* creates irreconciliation; as Crossan puts it, parable is the kind of story that brings not peace, but the sword. "Parables are meant to change, not reassure us."[4] Or put yet one more way, parables are unnerving. In the faith community, myth assures us, myth establishes our world, myth is necessary. Parable subverts our world.

Now you can imagine that this has been sliced and diced many ways to suggest that in the Church this thing or person represents myth and that thing or person functions as parabler. But it pleases me to think that while the presider in our assembly, the presbyters in the local church, focus the retelling of our core myth(s), the deacons are called to do some parablizing.

So many of Jesus' parables have been mythologized over the centuries. They have been treasured, translated, preached upon and sung about. I often challenge the deacons I teach and encourage them to try to recover some of the original shock value of the biblical parables. I also suggest they construct parables themselves, newly-spun stories with unexpected endings that shock, jar, provoke thought, and maybe even provoke change.

One more little point of which Crossan reminded us in his book is that it takes two to parable. We can each sit around by ourselves and recall myth(s). We can tell ourselves the stories which bind opposites together when we lie in bed at night, or when we meditate in the daytime. But for a parable to have the full impact of reversal, there must be a teller and hearers. Thus, parable is a community—two or three, at least, gathered together—event. When preaching on the parables in the Gospels or the parables in Hebrew scripture—Crossan notes Ruth and Jonah among the latter—we deacons must strive to bring a fresh note of surprise and reversal to them. When telling stories from our ministries in the wider community we must not sentimentalize or moralize them, or choose them for shock value alone, but for the energy of parable, the energy to challenge our hearers' accepted notions of what the world, and God's action in it, is like. In this way we participate in the Church's prophetic ministry.

I want to say a word about the difficulty of this role. It is challenging to speak a word to our communities, our towns and cities, and the institutions and associations in them. If we work in our gathered church communities, though, to build understanding not just of the issues we address but of how they connect to scripture, our traditions and our values, it is possible. It might even be relatively easy compared to speaking a word to the Church about its unjust acts and structures, its false values.

How difficult it is to risk a prophetic approach to an institution in which one is deeply embedded!

The example I have given repeatedly is from long ago and far away, in a diocese where activists proposed a resolution to the diocesan convention addressing a need for a living wage ordinance in its cities and counties. Leadership from a large congregation known for its progressive stances was key in this effort. But it turned out that the congregation contracted out its janitorial work to a company which did not pay even a minimum wage to its workers. No one wanted to hear this.

Even though it is difficult and risky, I think we deacons need to take heart, and when the opportunities come, not resist speaking out about these injustices and inconsistencies. If we do not point out our hypocrisies, someone who does not love the Church surely will.

Notes

1   For background see, for example, Kathryn Miles, "End of the Line", Globe Magazine, *Boston Globe*, 15 April 2018.

2   Ellen F. Davis, *Biblical Prophecy: Perspectives for Christian Theology, Discipleship and Ministry* (Louisville: Westminster John Knox Press, 2014), pp. 6–12.

3   Robert K. Greenleaf, *Servant Leadership* (New York: Paulist Press, 1977), p. 24.

4   John Dominic Crossan, *The Dark Interval: Toward a Theology of Story* (Sonoma: Polebridge Press, 1988), p. 39.

CHAPTER 13

Living the Prophetic Ministry of the Deacon

Gloria Marie Jones, OP

I begin with a quote by Deacon William Ditewig, someone who has contributed much to questions related to the diaconate and to whom I am indebted for his research and insights.[1] "Any conversation about the prophetic role of the deacon must be grounded in who we are as Church and what we are all called to be and to do as Church."

Vatican II initiated a new way of thinking about the Church and its ministerial roles. *Lumen gentium* identifies the Church as servant: a "kind of sacrament, a sign and an instrument of communion with God and of unity among all".[2] Pope Paul VI further amplified this message: "the Church has declared herself a servant of humanity . . . at the service of every condition, in every weakness and need".[3] Does that statement not point to a prophetic call, one that is shaped by the complex, challenging conditions of this moment in our world and by the critical needs of humanity which keep multiplying as we speak? If ever the Church was needed it is in this moment!

We know we possess *one* mission as Church: the mission of Jesus:

- his mission to announce, to make present, to fulfil God's desire that all people will come to know and experience, that God is here, one with them;
- that *all* is sacred, all peoples, all life;
- that in and through God's love made present in Jesus we are freed, forgiven, held in God's merciful love.

This is the mission for which the Church exists: to proclaim in word and in action the reign of God's love, mercy, forgiveness, peace in *every* culture, time and place, to *all* peoples.

Unfortunately, it is so easy for these words to lose their power, their challenge, and their significance with the passage of time. We can so easily get caught up in, distracted by, institutional complexities, by diversity of interpretations, by human frailty, ego and sin, paralyzed by power struggles and polarization. And the more we do so, the less we are who we are called to be. So where does the deacon and his prophetic call fit into this picture? We are back to the "being" and the "doing". At the heart of the deacon's ministry is the call to live, to make real in this moment the *kenosis*, the self-emptying love that is Jesus. The deacon is called to pour himself/herself out in service to the outcast, the marginalized, the poor and suffering, the crisis of our Earth, as Jesus did. Jesus didn't have an institution to worry about. His call was simply to share the truth of his Father's love, to incarnate his Father's love in his response to the people he encountered in the moment. Oh, to be so lucky!

That was Jesus and our call, our "doing". But we must never forget it was Jesus' communion with the Father that compelled him, that enabled him to pour himself out in love, to empty himself in service whatever the moment held; whether it was at the wedding feast at Cana, to the man born blind, to the woman caught in adultery, to the widow weeping for her deceased son, to the lepers, to the healing of the centurion's servant, to the woman at the well, to the feeding of the five thousand (we could go on and on), to the Last Supper, to the words of forgiveness as he hung on the cross and his ultimate, total outpouring of self, his *kenosis* on the cross. Whatever the moment held, his one passion was that the other would experience Abba's Love and be set free by that gift! Those are the footsteps in which the deacon walks. Cardinal Walter Kasper captured this call in these words:

> The basic attitude of the deacon must include a perceptive eye for those suffering distress, illness or fear. The task is to bring a healing that sets free and empowers them to trust and so to serve and Love others in their turn ... The goal of diaconal activity is not simply help, but the empowering of life, so that those who

> lie prostrate may get to their feet ... in some situations, the
> deacon can and must become the public advocate of the weak
> and powerless and of all those who have no other voice or lobby.[4]

This is prophetic ministry! *This is* the twofold mission of the deacon: to live in communion with God and pour herself/himself out in response to the needs of God's people. The deacon is called to live the *communio* and the *kenosis* of Jesus. Only in and through communion with God does servant leadership become real and true! "It is now not I who lives, but Christ Jesus who lives in me" (Galatians 2:20).

My reflection and prayer have led me to a deepened conviction: of all the ordained ministries, the diaconate is the one singularly poised to witness to the radical servant leadership of Jesus, which is at the heart of the prophetic call. The deacon can be most available to spend her/his energies to proclaim in word and action the reign of God in the concrete, immediate moment just as Jesus did.

The permanent diaconate sacramentalizes Jesus's call to *diakonia*. It sacramentalizes the call to be living signs of the servanthood of Christ's Church for all peoples.[5] This is particularly symbolized in the radical call to be foot-washers. Deacon William Ditewig articulates this challenging responsibility of deacons as a call to "leave security behind, strike out boldly, go into the deep. Risk everything for the sake of the gospel, give away their life". He goes on to say that

> our mission is to empty ourselves (*kenosis*) just as Christ has, to
> leave the comfort and security of the mountaintop for the rigors
> and messiness of life below, even to the point of giving our lives
> for others in imitation of Christ, our master.[6]

Might we also add: the deacon's mission is to leave the comfort and security of conformity to the social, political, religious expectation of others, the comfort of not rocking the boat, and instead to be deeply grounded in *communio* so as to be free to be a prophetic voice to the whole Church. We and our world need prophetic voices that are born from discerning hearts, grounded, centred in prayer/deep listening to the Spirit, focused on the mission of Jesus calling/challenging us as Church in this moment of time. Could that not be the grace of the diaconate to our Church today?

The integrity of the deacon's action, ministry, life is dependent on the quality of her/his personal relationship with groundedness in God. This is the one reality, the foundation that must shape all the deacon does. Your value, your worth is not determined by how much you know. It is not about how much you do. The most important, the essential focus for you is your commitment to your relationship with God, to wasting time with God, to know the truth of God's love for you, personally. It is so easy to get caught up in the demands of work, for prayer to be relegated to one more task that you must do! May you never forget that the source of your strength, your wisdom, your ministry, your preaching *is* the power of God's love, God's presence, God's life in you. Most important is your daily experience of being transformed by God's Word, to become one with God who feeds you in Eucharist, to be open to the God who meets you in silence, in darkness, in vulnerability. Your spiritual formation IS the foundation of your prophetic call.

I began with the statement that any conversation about the prophetic role of the deacon must be grounded in who we are as Church and what we are all called to be and to do as Church. The deacon's prophetic mission must be one with the prophetic mission of Jesus. Three profound beliefs shaped Jesus' prophetic mission; again and again we witness Jesus's prayer and preaching:

- that all shall be one, his prayer for *unity;*
- that all be welcomed at the table, his witness to *inclusivity;*
- that all are forgiven, his commitment to *compassion and forgiveness.*

The prophetic mission of Jesus, and therefore of the deacon, is about unity, inclusivity and forgiveness. What great need there is for these three gifts in our Church, in our communities, in our world!

I have to confess my reflection and prayer stirred up great discomfort within me. How much we struggle within the Roman Catholic Church with unity, inclusivity and forgiveness. How much we struggle among our Christian churches with unity, inclusivity and forgiveness. How much we struggle in our social and political worlds with unity, inclusivity and forgiveness.

What witness does our Church give to this reality? In truth, there is polarization and division within our US Catholic Church, among the US Catholic hierarchy, among religious women. It is a scandal eroding our integrity. *All* of us who have given our lives, who are consecrated to the service of Jesus and his kingdom through the ministry and life of the Church—all ordained ministers, deacons, priests, bishops, all religious men and women—have a serious obligation, a responsibility to direct our energy, our work, our prayer, our preaching, our outreach to Jesus' call to unity, inclusivity and forgiveness! Such a commitment is prophetic! Such a commitment is transformative!

I dare to say that relegating this radical call to some peripheral agenda or, worse, simply giving lip-service to it without taking seriously the cost and embracing the challenge, is part of our institutional sin. Each of us has a fundamental responsibility to be instruments of unity, inclusivity and forgiveness right where we find ourselves, within our own institutions, within our faith communities, in the context of our daily lives. None of us can change the world or our diocese or the problems of our community, but we can make a difference in this moment, whatever it holds, by the witness of our lives to unity, inclusivity and forgiveness.

I have had a special grace of being part of the Nuns and Nones movement in the United States. The movement is bringing together religious women and millennials from all faiths/non-faiths and walks of life. These are young people searching for answers and for people to walk with them. Their questions, their needs and desires have inspired me. They talk about longing to live in intentional communities; they are asking us sisters to teach them about living in community. They are seeking spiritual practices that nurture their spirits, that can lead them to peace and wisdom and inner strength. They want to know about our spiritual practices, about what nurtures our spirits. They are longing to find a way to live in our world that is not driven by the values of power and money, and exploitation. They are looking to us, religious women, because they see in our lives choices that have created another way of being in the world. The majority of them are not connected with an institutional faith experience. The sadness is that so many institutions hold "too much baggage" for them. And yet, I experience the Spirit drawing them into the values of the kingdom of God. To what might the Spirit be calling us through them?

We are challenged to fierce honesty and soulful discernment, individually and institutionally, that we might be attentive to where the Spirit is meeting us, calling us to new life, to ever greater integrity. This is a journey we cannot make alone. We need each other to be faithful. What a difference it would make, how prophetic it would truly be to unite our energies, our commitment, to focus our priorities to create communities shaped by unity, inclusivity and forgiveness! To proclaim in word and action God is here, all is sacred, grace abounds.

What a gift our deacons can be, what a gift they can bring to our Church by fanning the flame of this consciousness, through their lives, their *communio* and *kenosis*, their presence in our Church! We need them to BE this prophetic ministry!

May it be so!

Notes

[1]   Of special note is *The Emerging Diaconate: Servant Leaders in a Servant Church* (New York: Paulist Press, 2007).

[2]   *Lumen gentium* 1.

[3]   Paul VI, *Hodie concilium*, *Acta Apostolicae Sedis* 58 (1966), pp. 57–64.

[4]   Walter Kasper, "The Diaconate", in *Leadership in the Church: How Traditional Roles Can Serve the Christian Community Today* (New York: Crossroad, 2003), p. 40.

[5]   See Congregation for Catholic Education, *Basic Norms for the Formation of Permanent Deacons* (Vatican City: Libreria Editrice Vaticana, 1998), and the *National Directory*.

[6]   William T. Ditewig, *To Be and To Serve: The Ministerial Identity of the Deacon*, Location 254 of 437 Kindle book.

PART 6

The Deacon in the Worshipping Community

CHAPTER 14

The Deacon in Worship: A Ministry of Hospitality

Rosalind Brown

The story of the resurrection appearance on the Emmaus Road is a story of reciprocal hospitality: just when the disciples thought they were the hosts of a stranger, Jesus was revealed as their host. We sing of this extraordinary truth in the hymn, "Come, risen Lord, and deign to be our guest; nay, let us be thy guests, this feast is thine". If Jesus is our host at every celebration of the Eucharist, offering God's hospitality to us, then I want to work with the idea that—to borrow John Collins' contribution—the deacon is the butler, the head-servant, who acts on behalf of the owner of a large household. And so, in this chapter, I explore the idea of the deacon as the person who arranges the hospitality at the Eucharist, the Mass.

The Last Supper was Jesus' final act of hospitality to his disciples, hospitality first offered when he invited two of them to "come and see" where he was staying and they stayed all day. I wonder what they talked about and what they ate. Jesus was a cook. I am struck by the words that go unremarked in Mark's Gospel, when the disciples asked Jesus where they should go to make the Passover preparations. Jesus' reply suggests that he, unbeknown to his companions, had made meticulous preparations in advance. Usually women, not men, carried water jars in public so, in the heightened tension around his presence in Jerusalem, this could have been a careful plan to identify the person they were to follow. And the room was furnished and ready: Jesus had made the arrangements to host his friends; the advance party just had to make the final preparations.

That is hospitality, as was his action on the beach that unforgettable resurrection morning, when he had breakfast on the go when they needed it. His choice of charcoal meant the smell would take Peter back to the charcoal fire by which he had denied Jesus a few days earlier and thus facilitate the subsequent conversation when Jesus, by giving Peter the chance to rework that failure, enabled Peter to know that he was truly and forever welcome. Jesus as host was very attentive to detail. Incidentally, it can be interesting to ask people if they can imagine Jesus in charge of a barbecue; for some it's a startling thought. Reflecting on Jesus' hospitality, I once wrote:

> O God of feast and festival,
> of water turned to wine,
> you fed the crowds who followed you,
> with outcasts chose to dine;
> gregarious God, your acts reveal
> a place for us at every meal.
>
> O God of family and home,
> of simple times with friends,
> you breakfast-cook at Galilee,
> companion when day ends;
> endearing God, your acts reveal
> how gently love and care can heal.
>
> O God who walked Emmaus Road
> and joined in Cana's feast,
> at times you slip into our lives
> when we expect you least;
> surprising God, your acts reveal
> what your appearance may conceal.

O God of hospitality,
still welcoming us all,
you also come through those in need,
the inconvenient call;
O God, let all our acts reveal
the welcome that from you we feel.[1]

So I'd like to explore the deacon's role in worship as one of offering hospitality. And that, perhaps inevitably, takes me to St Benedict. For thirteen years I served in what was, for 450 years, a Benedictine monastic cathedral, and we still tried to live by Benedict's principles. When Benedict wrote, travel left people vulnerable to the perils on unmade roads and was physically exhausting, so visitors arrived tired and hungry from a substantial journey. Benedict's principle? "All guests who present themselves are to be welcomed as Christ, who said 'I was a stranger and you welcomed me'".[2] That doesn't just mean treating guests well, but expecting to meet Christ when we greet someone at the door. How might that possibility affect how we approach them? Joan Chittister writes pithily:

Of all the questions to be asked . . . one of the most pointed must surely be why one of the great spiritual documents of the Western world would have in it a chapter on how to answer the door. And one of the answers might be that answering the door is one of the arch-activities of Benedictine life. The way we answer doors is the way we deal with the world. . . . The chapter on the porter of the monastery is the chapter on how to receive the Christ in the other, always.[3]

In my book *Being a Deacon Today*, I suggested that deacons should be freed from other duties in church before a service, so that they can be on the church doorstep, welcoming people and helping them over the threshold which for some people could feel like an enormous hurdle to be jumped, even threatening. Think of your own church door: how easy is it to find and to open, especially if you are nervous? Is the entrance area welcoming?

A colleague once asked a group of church members in his previous parish—some long-standing, some very new—to review the church's ministry of hospitality. When they reported back, the problem was identified as the church door. So what to do about it? Their answer was not a new door but to put a "welcome" outside the door who would open the door for everyone—not just visitors—and help them over the threshold. Flannery O'Connor has written, "Most of us come to the church by a means that the church does not allow."[4]

Deacons, through their ministry beyond church doors during the week, are on the doorstep to make sure that the many surprising ways to the church are kept open and people are encouraged to take them. So if a church has a deacon, that is where he or she should be, because welcoming people is the first role of the deacon in worship, echoed by the presider in the opening greeting. Deacons can also train other welcomers to understand this as part of the liturgy.

Hospitality finds a welcome for everyone at their own level, and some people need space to sit on the fringes and not be drawn in too far. There are always people sitting at the back of Durham Cathedral during services who are welcome to be there and to come and go. I realize it is not always as easy in churches where there is not the same space that the Cathedral has. But this may be a person's first time, and they want to see what goes on before deciding whether to be drawn in. My equivalent of their vulnerability of suddenly being immersed in a strange new world with very different norms would be visiting a casino. I wouldn't have a clue what to do, so initially would need to observe from the sidelines, feeling out of my depth unless someone came alongside me to help. So hospitality bids us put a deacon on the church door to welcome and reassure people, not just to hand out a pile of books or notice sheets. Incidentally, at the Cathedral we identify books by their colour, because saying "the hymn book" or "the prayer book" is meaningless to some visitors. At the same time, the deacon can welcome the regulars, some of whom live alone and may not have spoken to anyone for days, and can pick up needs to be woven into the church's prayers or provide the catalyst for a home visit.

So the deacon offers hospitality on the church doorstep, inviting people to worship. This continues in the formal liturgy as the deacon invites people to clear their consciences with God and, like Peter on the seashore, to put their failures behind them and know that they are forgiven and can hold their heads up in God's presence. The deacon offers the people the hospitality of the gospel, God's good news of his incarnational and transforming presence among us—at times in centuries past guarding those precious gospel scrolls and books literally with their life. And the gospel must be heard clearly: Benedict was firm that readers must be able to edify their hearers,[5] and learning to read well in public is a diaconal duty.

Then, in leading the intercessions, deacons are agents of hospitality for the woes and worries, joys and hopes of the world which people bring to worship, enabling them to find their rightful place in the worship, neither dominating it nor being ignored. Very often at the Cathedral we are thanked for our intercessions, because the words have been hospitable. Well-led intercessions give people a vocabulary with which to pray, expressing needs they feel deeply but cannot always put into their own words.

Bidding people share the Peace, when we recognize one another as the reconciled body of Christ, leads into the deacon setting the Table around which we all gather. Benedict's description of the monastery cellarer is pertinent here.[6] The cellarer is responsible to take care not only of things, like food and kitchen utensils, but in doing so to care for people who have crossed the threshold of the monastery. He or she is to be humble and to ensure their words and actions do not lead little ones astray, and we can include vulnerable adults in that.

As an aside, Benedict's approach, of seeing diaconal ministry as caring for people, applies to setting the altar but also to how we serve food or do the washing up at refreshments after the service. Ladling soup or pouring tea at a soup kitchen or parish lunch can be done in many ways, not all of them hospitably. Benedict says that the vessels on the altar are to be treated in the same way as the kitchen utensils of the monastery, to which he gives special attention.[7] At Durham Cathedral, we put some extracts from the Rule on the kitchen cupboards, along with a twenty-first-century interpretation, because, in a community that offers hospitality and where many people use the kitchen, it is important that the equipment people need is on hand. We struggle with this, as plates and cutlery seem to have legs of their own, which just shows how timeless is Benedict's wisdom.

It is not hospitable to the volunteers serving refreshments if things have been borrowed and not returned or the cups needed for coffee are still dirty in the sink, or there are no clean tea towels. With so many churches offering hospitality after worship, oversight of the kitchen and the rotas to provide hospitality can be seen as an element of the deacon's ministry of hospitality in worship and engagement with the community.

So here is Benedict on the subject of care of the utensils that keep the monastery running, whether in the kitchen, the garden or the sacristy:

> For the care of the monastery's property in tools, clothing and other articles let the Abbess appoint sisters on whose manner of life and character she can rely; and let her, as she shall judge to be expedient, consign the various articles to them, to be looked after and to be collected again.[8]

Notice that anyone in charge of utensils must have a reliable manner of life and character, just as the doorkeeper's qualifications include wisdom and maturity.[9] These are important duties and not to be assigned lightly, hence—extrapolating to ordained ministry—the bishop's questioning of the character of those to be ordained.

Both setting the table and clearing up are vital parts of hospitality, whether offered at home or in the Eucharist, which is the expression of our Lord's hospitality to us. So the deacon prepares the altar for the eucharistic celebration. One child visiting Durham Cathedral in a school group saw the high altar and asked the guide, "Is that tablecloth like my Mam puts out when we have a special meal?" She'd got the message: special altar linens matter. Kathleen Norris' book *The Cloister Walk* tells of her experiences as a "married woman with a thoroughly Protestant background and often more doubt than faith",[10] when she spent two extended residencies in a Roman Catholic Benedictine monastery. In another article about this experience, she describes an epiphany moment in the Mass of seeing a vested minister, quite possibly a deacon, doing the ablutions at the altar. I couldn't find the quotation where she records her astonishment that (in my recollection of her words) "he was doing the washing up in the service!", which led her to realize how the work she did at her kitchen sink day in, day out, for her family has immense value in God's sight and is not out of place on the altar at the end of the Mass. Deacons model holding together Church and world.

And then the deacon is back to directing traffic over the church doorstep as, with the Dismissal, the deacon orders rather than invites people to leave church to live in the world the new way of eucharistic living of which they have had a foretaste in church. And if the deacon can do that by demonstrating the value of washing up, of care of utensils, of proclaiming the gospel, of bringing the needs of the world into the heart of worship, then maybe, just maybe, the gathered and worshipping people of God will catch a vision of how they can offer Christ's hospitality to the people they meet in the coming week. In other words, how they, led by the deacon, can bring eucharistic life and worship into the heart of the world.

Notes

[1]   Copyright © 1995 Rosalind Brown.

[2]   The Rule of St Benedict, Chapter 53.

[3]   Joan Chittister, *The Rule of Benedict: Insights for the Ages* (New York: Crossroad, 1992), p. 170.

[4]   Kathleen Norris, *Dakota: A Spiritual Geography* (Boston: Houghton Mifflin Company, 1993), p. 63.

[5]   The Rule of St Benedict, Chapter 38.

[6]   The Rule of St Benedict, Chapter 31.

[7]   The Rule of St Benedict, Chapter 31.

[8]   The Rule of St Benedict, Chapter 32.

[9]   The Rule of St Benedict, Chapter 66.

[10] Kathleen Norris, *The Cloister Walk* (New York: Riverhead Books, 1996), inside front cover.

CHAPTER 15

Attentiveness: The Liturgy in the Spiritual Life of the Deacon

Frederick C. Bauerschmidt

Ordination to the diaconate brings with it a relationship of the deacon to the Church's liturgy and the liturgical assembly that often poses a spiritual challenge to deacons, particularly the newly-ordained. I want to focus on two specific challenges. First, there is the challenge posed by a shift in role within the liturgical assembly that the deacon experiences, from being one of the assembly of the faithful to being, as it were, the *major domo* of that assembly. Second, there is the challenge posed by the expectation that one's personal prayer will take on a distinctively liturgical quality, specifically the daily recitation of the Liturgy of the Hours. These challenges, properly understood, can be an opportunity for a growth in spiritual depth. They can also, however, lead to a deadly spiritual malaise.

First, the challenge of being the liturgical *major domo* (the phrase is taken from Aidan Kavanagh). As the name suggests, the deacon is the servant of the liturgical assembly (not, as some might assume, the servant of the priest–celebrant). Of course, this is true, or should be true, of all liturgical ministries. Ministers are there to ensure that the assembly's worship is carried out with dignity and a certain ease, which allows the baptized to engage in the serious work of worshipping almighty God. But like the head of a large household (think of Carson in *Downton Abbey*), the deacon serves in a special way by exercising care not only over his or her own service, but also over everyone else's service. You might say that the deacon's ministry—and this does not apply solely to liturgical ministry—is one of care for the ministry of others. This typically means that it is the deacon who worries about those technicalities concerning who does what, when, where and how. It is the deacon who must anticipate the unforeseeable by keeping a sharp eye out for ants in chalices, flaming altar servers, mismarked books and confused celebrants. To make matters worse, the nature of the liturgical assembly is such that deacons cannot simply take all tasks upon themselves. That would be far too easy. No, because the diversity of ministries in the liturgical assembly mirrors the diversity of gifts within the body of Christ and the deacon must try to manage liturgies in which a variety of people with varying degrees of skill and aptitude are reading and singing and serving and distributing Communion. The deacon must do this in a way that is unobtrusive, not hovering distrustfully over the other ministers of the liturgy but giving them the freedom to fulfil their ministries.

It is perhaps no surprise that the shift from being someone who just needs to remember that we now say "And with your spirit" instead of "And also with you", to being someone who must know not only the deacon's words and actions but also the words and actions of every minister in the liturgy, can be a stressful one. Often deacons feel that they have lost the ability to pray during the liturgy, because they are so concerned with making sure that things run smoothly. They cannot let themselves get swept up in the liturgical action because they have to make sure that the action itself is moving forward. And in this concern, it is possible to let trivialities distract us from the experience of the liturgy itself. I know myself that many a Sunday, during the Eucharistic Prayer, my mind will wander to important matters like whether we have enough wine in the chalices, or if the ushers are aware of the bird that has just flown in through the main doors, or how can I discreetly tell the altar server behind me to stop twirling his damned cincture—and then suddenly I realize that the consecration has happened, and I have once again missed the moment.

Particularly if you have a strong affective attachment to the liturgy, if you are one who is deeply moved during worship, you must master your emotions, because you've got a job to do. You cannot have a spiritual reverie during the elevation of the host, because you may have to be getting ready to remove the pall from the chalice. You cannot engage in pious practices like striking your breast during the *Agnus Dei*, because you may

need to be arranging the vessels for the distribution of Communion. At
the same time, if the deacon's approach to serving the liturgical assembly
is mechanistic and robotic, entirely consumed with making sure the
liturgy is "correct", then he or she is not effectively serving the assembly.
Un-prayerful briskness in carrying out diaconal duties is as destructive
of the assembly's prayer as is sloppy or chaotic ritual. So one must find
a way of *being* prayerful—not just *appearing* prayerful, since people can
sense when you're faking it—a way of genuinely immersing yourself in
the divine reality being celebrated, whilst at the same time immersing
yourself in the minutiae of the ritual. In other words, one must find a way
to make one's liturgical *diakonia* itself an act of prayer.

The mid-twentieth-century philosopher Simone Weil wrote of the role
of "attention" in the spiritual life, in her "Reflections on the Right Use
of School Studies with a View to the Love of God", in *Waiting for God*.[1]
She suggested that tedious and even failed attempts at solving geometry
proofs or learning a language could cultivate in us a capacity for attention,
and that attention, when directed toward God, "is the very substance of
prayer".[2] Weil describes attention as "an effort, the greatest of all effort
perhaps, but," she says, "it is a negative effort".[3] This effort is the work of
waiting: "We do not obtain the most precious gifts by going in search of
them but by waiting for them."[4] Weil says that a servant may labour all
day long and yet remain an unprofitable servant (Matthew 17:10); what
makes the master love the servant "is only watching, waiting, attention".[5]

The deacon's role in the liturgy might be thought of as one of attentive
concern for the entire ensemble of word and song and gesture that
constitutes the liturgical action. The ministry of the deacon is not one of
strenuous control of the liturgical assembly, but the service that consists
in watching, waiting, attention. If the deacon understands his or her role
as the minister to the ministers of the assembly in this way, then attentive
concern paid to the liturgical action is not a hindrance to prayer but,
as Weil puts it, "the very substance of prayer". The deacon's ministry is
at its heart not a matter of rigid enforcement of rubrical prescriptions
(as important as those rubrics might be), but of waiting to see what the
Spirit might do next, and making sure that the assembly is able to forget
itself in attentive waiting upon the Spirit. Of course, one will still need
to deal with ants in the chalice and confused celebrants, and one may

often feel at the end of the liturgy as if one has not prayed, but prayer is about more than feeling.

If prayer is truly about attention, then perhaps the practice of liturgical attentiveness that is at the heart of the deacon's ministry might bear fruit in his or her private prayer. Which brings me to the second challenge that I mentioned at the outset: the challenge of much of one's prayer life being made up of prescribed liturgical forms. At least in the Roman Catholic context, ordination brings with it the obligation to pray some part of the Liturgy of the Hours; for deacons, in my experience, this usually means Morning and Evening Prayer. This of course does not preclude other forms of prayer, such as *lectio divina* or the rosary or centring prayer, but, given the fact that many deacons also have families and secular jobs, it seems likely that a significant part of the deacon's prayer life will consist of the official prayer of the Church.

This poses a challenge to some deacons for at least two reasons. First, the Liturgy of the Hours, unlike the relatively fixed form of the Mass, manages to be both complicated and tedious. It is not by accident that the four volumes of the Liturgy of the Hours each come with five ribbons, which often prove insufficient for those days when one has, say, the feast of an apostle in Eastertime. Many deacons have turned to online versions of the Hours that present all of the texts of the day in one place as a remedy to the office's complexity, though I myself have some doubts about the benefits of reading off a screen for the life of prayer. At the same time, for all of its complexity, the office, over time, is highly repetitive. The psalter, which makes up the bulk of the office in the Roman Rite, is the same every four weeks and, last time I checked, no one is writing any new psalms. If one adds to this the fact that most deacons pray the Hours most of the time by themselves, without any music, it can make for a fairly drab diet.

Second, many deacons are never taught *how* to pray the Liturgy of the Hours. I do not mean by this that they are not told about the mechanics of the four-week psalter, or the difference between a memorial and an optional memorial, or to make the sign of the cross at the beginning of the Gospel canticles. These things are undoubtedly covered. They are often not taught, however, how to pray ancient texts like the psalms, which often seem focused on late Bronze Age politics or expressing feelings of personal spite at unnamed enemies. What they are not taught is how to read such texts spiritually, as the Church Fathers did, so that prayers for the peace of Jerusalem can become prayers for peace in one's soul, or thanksgiving for God's mighty act at the Red Sea can become thanksgiving for our own passing over from death to life in baptism. What they are not taught is how to turn the word of God into the bread of life that can nourish their souls. If one combines the repetitiveness of the psalter with an inability to penetrate to its depths, one begins to get an idea of how the Liturgy of the Hours might become a burden.

Here again, I think Simone Weil's idea of attentiveness as the very substance of prayer is of use. The Church Fathers' practice of "spiritual reading" required a particular kind of attention to the text, not the strenuous attention of the modern exegete, but rather openness to letting the text penetrate and permeate their souls. This is not a matter of grasping each word, but of letting ourselves be grasped by the word. It is a matter of living with the tedium of waiting for the Spirit to speak through the letter, not by trying to control our mental focus, which will only lead to spiritual exhaustion, but by letting desire for the Spirit's speaking guide our attention. Just as the deacon must learn attentive openness in ministering in the public liturgies of the Church, so too the deacon must apply the same attentiveness in praying the Church's prayer.

Simone Weil concludes her reflections on attention and the love of God by noting, "Not only does the love of God have attention for its substance; the love of neighbour, which we know to be the same love, is made of the same substance." She notes that "the capacity to give one's attention to a sufferer is a very rare and difficult thing; it is almost a miracle; it *is* a miracle".[6] This suggests how the capacity for attention might link the deacon's ministry of liturgy to the deacon's ministry of charity. The attentiveness that we exercise and cultivate in both public and private prayer should enlarge our compassion, our capacity to see the sufferers of the world. The charism of attentiveness should be the link between our ministry at the altar and our ministry in the world.

Notes

[1]   Simone Weil, *Waiting for God* (New York: Harper & Row, 1973).

[2]   Ibid., p. 106.

[3]   Ibid., p. 111.

[4]   Ibid., p. 112.

[5]   Ibid., p. 114.

[6]   Ibid., p. 114.

CHAPTER 16

Appreciating the Liturgical Role of the Deacon

D. Michael Jackson

I approach this topic as an Anglican appreciating the Roman Catholic view of the liturgical ministry of the deacon. Here I see three dimensions:

- Clear, firm and comprehensive direction for diaconal participation in the Eucharist, given in *The General Instruction of the Roman Missal*;
- Excellent publications on the deacon in the liturgy; and
- The underlying historical, theological and pastoral rationale for the diaconal role in worship.

Let me focus on this third point before looking at some specific examples of where Anglicans and Episcopalians could benefit from Roman Catholic theory and practice.

Rationale for the deacon in worship

We must ask ourselves a basic question: is the liturgical role of the deacon essential or even important? The Anglican response to this is ambivalent, to say the least. The Roman Catholic answer, on the other hand, is unequivocal: the ministry of the deacon is grounded in the worship, sacraments and spirituality of the Church. On this subject I commend *The Character of the Deacon: Spiritual and Pastoral Foundations*, a book of essays edited by Deacon James Keating. Let me quote the very first words of his Introduction:

> The deacon's primary ministry is twofold: to serve at the altar and ambo and from such service be sent by Christ, while always abiding with him in prayer, to respond to the spiritual and corporeal needs of people.[1]

The role of the deacon is based on the sacramental identity given through ordination. It is tripartite: word, liturgy and charity. As one contributor to *The Character of the Deacon* neatly puts it, they are "three atoms united in a single molecular ministry". Without the sacramental grace conferred through ordination, the deacon "would be a social organizer but not a divine minister".[2] Another contributor says, "our service is not sufficient if it is reduced to social service [. . .] diaconal spirituality originates in the liturgy and points to service in the church and the world".[3] Roman Catholic scholars take care to balance the spiritual and practical dimensions of the diaconate. Adding an Eastern perspective, an Orthodox bishop and theologian contends that "*diakonia* involves not only mercy, justice, and prophecy, but also worship, upbuilding the church, royal priesthood, and prayer and intercession".[4]

This can be a useful reminder, and indeed a corrective, for those emphasizing social activism to the detriment, even the exclusion, of the deacon's ministry of Word and sacrament. The Australian Roman Catholic scholar John N. Collins has challenged the long-accepted consensus that the Greek word *diakonia* meant humble service. The term, argues Collins, meant much more than that, certainly in its Pauline usage—commissioned minister, ambassador, intermediary, mediator, agent of the bishop. . .[5] He traces the prevailing modern view of the diaconate to the strong influence of the Lutheran Churches in Germany, where since the nineteenth century *diakonia* has been equated with charitable service.[6] (Other contributors to this volume pick up on the issue of diaconal identity raised by Collins.[7])

This hitherto long-accepted consensus about the function of the diaconate may help explain a trend in the Anglican and Episcopal churches in North America to devalue, depreciate or ignore the liturgical—and, I might add, the preaching—role of the deacon, in order to emphasize a prophetic diaconal ministry of justice. In some Canadian dioceses, the deacon's role in worship is minimized, downplayed or even discouraged. This appears to be for two reasons:

1. The reluctance of priest-presiders to cede part of their liturgical roles to deacons; and
2. The view that the deacon's liturgical functions detract from lay ministry (to this we add a corollary, especially in the Church of England, that they compete with lay readers).

So we still face (1) the spectre of the one-man (or woman) -band presbyter in liturgy, and (2) the old straw man (or woman!) of the deacon taking away from lay involvement. Let me firmly assert the contrary: that the liturgical role of the deacon has sound historical and theological bases; it does not threaten anyone; and every deacon should fulfil it in his/her parish.

The view that the deacon's role in worship is peripheral is reflected in the 2016 *Iona Report* on the diaconate in the Anglican Church of Canada.[8] Of the twenty pages dealing with competencies for the diaconate, only a half-page is devoted to the liturgical role, and in a very perfunctory and incomplete manner. The preaching function is barely mentioned. If this became the prevailing view in the Anglican Church, we would be looking at the deacon as an ecclesiastical social worker. That is a very worthwhile vocation indeed—but it does not require the sacramental identity conferred by ordination. A deacon colleague in the Diocese of Qu'Appelle made a very pertinent observation in a response to the *Iona Report*:

> "Word" and "service" are descriptors of the liturgical function of the deacon and, as such, cannot be understood as foundational to the diaconal ministry apart from it. The liturgy, and God's spirit within it, calls us again and again back to our vows, reminds us of our vocational call, teaches us who we are to be amidst and among the whole people of God, and only then sends us out into the world to continue that worship and work in the world.[9]

Now, I hasten to add that I am not promoting the deacon as just a liturgical functionary! Rightly, dioceses introducing diaconal programmes discourage candidates who see themselves in this light. An example is the Roman Catholic Diocese of Saskatoon, which has been very cautious in accepting the permanent diaconate, precisely for this reason. We need a harmonious balance of the diaconal ministries of word, liturgy and charity. I cite two examples of this balance: Christ Church Cathedral (Anglican) in Victoria, where Nancy Ford's extensive social ministry as deacon to the city is rooted in her preaching and liturgical ministry; and Holy Rosary Cathedral (Roman Catholic) in Regina, where Deacon Barry Wood preaches monthly and assists at the liturgy while undertaking prison ministry and earning his living as archdiocesan financial officer.

The deacon in the *Roman Missal*

For Anglicans and Episcopalians, the *General Instruction for the Roman Missal* must seem perplexing, even alien. It would be unthinkable for centralized authority in one of our national churches, let alone internationally, to decree norms for rite, ceremony, vesture and furnishings. But that is what the missal does, to the benefit of the liturgical role of the deacon. The *General Instruction* specifies the deacon's functions in the eucharistic rite, to the extent that it provides for two options: mass with a deacon and mass without a deacon. Let me quote a key passage:

> After the Priest, the Deacon, in virtue of the sacred Ordination he has received, holds first place among those who minister in the celebration of the Eucharist. [. . .] At Mass the Deacon has his own part in proclaiming the Gospel, from time to time in preaching God's Word, in announcing the intentions of the Universal Prayer, in ministering to the Priest, in preparing the altar and in serving the celebration of the Sacrifice, in distributing the Eucharist to the faithful, especially under the species of wine, and from time to time in giving instructions regarding the people's gestures and postures.[10]

This is a succinct and yet complete description of the deacon's role at the Eucharist. One could only wish that something similar appeared in Anglican prayer books! The *General Instruction* gives detailed directions for diaconal participation:

- It describes the entrance rite, the proclaiming of the Gospel, the general intercession, the preparation of the altar, the communion and the ablutions.
- It specifies who does what in the absence of a deacon. For example, only an assisting priest or the presiding celebrant may proclaim the Gospel, something Anglican prayer books do not mention.
- Mercifully, the Roman rite does not provide for processing the Gospel reading down the centre aisle of the church, a custom introduced in the American Episcopal Church in the 1950s and which my late mentor, Deacon Ormonde Plater, deplored.
- The deacon "says the invitation to the Sign of Peace" ("let us offer each other the sign of peace"). Anglican books do not include this—but Ormonde Plater recommended that Anglican and Episcopal deacons do it anyway!
- After Communion, the deacon is assigned the responsibility of consuming the remaining bread and wine and purifying the vessels—again, something which is absent from the Anglican rites.
- The Roman rite makes specific provision for the preaching ministry of the deacon as a norm, which Anglican liturgies fail to do.

Now, in fairness to Anglican liturgists, both the 1979 American Episcopal *Book of Common Prayer* and the 1985 Canadian *Book of Alternative Services* are very deacon-friendly—they were in fact well ahead of their time. They make full provision for the diaconal role not only in the Eucharist, but in Holy Week and other special services, pastoral services and episcopal liturgies. They could simply benefit from including the points just mentioned.

The Church of England is another story. Its *Alternative Service Book* of 1980 virtually ignores the deacon. *Common Worship* of 2000 is not much better. While it does refer to the deacon's liturgical role, it does so half-heartedly:

> In some traditions the ministry of the deacon at Holy Communion has included some of the following elements: the bringing in of the Book of the Gospels, the invitation to confession, the reading of the Gospel, the preaching of the sermon when licensed to do so, a part of the prayers of intercession, the preparation of the table and the gifts, a part in the distribution, the ablutions and the dismissal.

This is actually a good description of the diaconal function in the Eucharist, as far as it goes. But then comes a disclaimer:

> The deacon's liturgical ministry provides an appropriate model for the ministry of an assisting priest, a reader, or another episcopally authorized minister in a leadership ministry that complements that of the president.[11]

For the Church of England, the diaconal role in worship appears to be an optional appendage.

Publications on the diaconate

Let me pay tribute to Roman Catholic scholars and writers on the liturgical role of the deacon. They are firmly grounded in the history, tradition and theology of the diaconate, yet they are user-friendly, sensible, practical and on occasion humorous. They rank with the revered Episcopal scholar, Deacon Ormonde Plater. Let me indulge in some of my favourite quotes:

William T. Ditewig writes that while it is "important to know *what* a deacon does at Mass, it is even more important to understand *why* the deacon does it".[12]

Michael Kwatera writes of the "complementary ministries of the priest and deacon [. . .] As deacons minister within the liturgy, they are a clear sign that the liturgy does not belong to the presiding priest alone."[13]

Frederick C. Bauerschmidt: When raising the chalice at the doxology, the deacon "ought to hold the chalice in two hands, so as not to look as if he is offering a toast".[14]

W. Shawn McKnight: "The image of the master of ceremonies in the liturgy serves as a good analogy of what the ministry of the deacon should look like in the Church [. . .] [The deacon] prepares, anticipates, directs, encourages, and helps the entire assembly to fulfil their functions with grace. He is the *designated worrier* [my italics] for the assembly, which relies upon him when the unexpected occurs."[15]

Frederick C. Bauerschmidt: "As the liturgy's principal servant, the deacon needs to cultivate a keen sense of 'situational awareness', knowing at all times who should be doing what—whether this be the presider, readers, altar servers or extraordinary ministers of Holy Communion—and helping them to do what they are supposed to do without appearing in any way to usurp their ministries."[16]

Ormonde Plater: "Deacons serve best when they dare, when they speak out and act out, when they get themselves and others in trouble—even when they arouse the mob".[17] When preaching, "[d]eacons are the chief aggravators in the congregation—or they should be—and they don't have to worry about pleasing people".[18]

And finally, Dennis Smolarski, SJ: "Priests should not dress like deacons, ever."[19]

Communion from the Reserved Sacrament

Let me address a final point regarding the liturgical ministry of the deacon: presiding at services of Communion from the reserved sacrament. This is frowned on in some Anglican dioceses and forbidden in others. Maylanne Maybee questions the so-called "deacon's mass" in a chapter in this book.[20] But let me make a plea for the value and validity of this ministry, when a priest is not available and people are desirous of receiving Holy Communion in church.

Our Roman Catholic friends once again give us guidance. Michael Kwatera does not consider "Holy Communion outside Mass" to be in any way "a poor substitute for the Mass" but a valid if temporary alternative in the absence of a priest for the "ideal form of Sunday worship".[21] Both he and Frederick Bauerschmidt offer helpful suggestions for the deacon–presider. Says Deacon Bauerschmidt, "part of the challenge for deacons presiding at these celebrations is to honor the sense of absence they convey, while still helping the assembly to celebrate the presence of the risen Christ".[22]

Anglicans are increasingly a eucharistic worshipping community. In my own experience in both a city church and a seasonal rural one, many of our people are reluctant to fall back on Morning Prayer for Sunday worship when a priest is not available. Services of the Word with Communion from the reserved sacrament, if they are carefully prepared, clearly explained and sensitively conducted, can be spiritually meaningful and pastorally effective. They should be considered a legitimate form of diaconal ministry.

———

Let me conclude with a word from the inimitable Deacon Ormonde Plater. When asked about ambivalence and hesitation over what the deacon should do in the liturgy, he responded, "My motto: When in doubt, do it!"[23]

Notes

[1] James Keating (ed.), *The Character of the Deacon: Spiritual and Pastoral Foundations* (New York: Paulist Press, 2017), p. xi.

[2] David W. Fagerberg, "The *Lex Orandi* of the Ordination Rite", in Keating (ed.), *The Character of the Deacon*, pp. 111, 116.

[3] Stephen F. Miletic, "The Mystery of Jesus as Deacon", in Keating (ed.), *The Character of the Deacon*, p. 36.

[4] Paulos Mar Gregorios, *The Meaning and Nature of Diakonia* (Geneva: World Council of Churches, 1988), quoted in Ormonde Plater, *Many Servants: An Introduction to Deacons*, Revised Edition (Cambridge, MA: Cowley Publications, 2004), p. xii.

5   *Diakonia: Re-interpreting the Ancient Sources* (New York, Oxford: Oxford University Press, 1990) and *Deacons and the Church: Making Connections Between Old and New* (Leominster: Gracewing; Harrisburg, PA: Morehouse, 2002).

6   See the most recent book by John N. Collins, *Diakonia Studies: Critical Issues in Ministry* (New York, Oxford: Oxford University Press, 2014), especially Chapters 11, 12, 14.

7   Frederick C. Bauerschmidt, "The Deacon and Sacramental Character"; Rosalind Brown, "Theological Underpinnings of the Diaconate"; Maylanne Maybee, "The Diaconate as Ecumenical Opportunity".

8   *The Iona Report: The Diaconate in the Anglican Church of Canada* (Toronto: The General Synod of the Anglican Church of Canada, October 2016), <https://www.anglican.ca/faith/ministry/om/diaconate/>.

9   Krista Dowdeswell, "Response to the Iona Report: The Diaconate in the Anglican Church of Canada", Diocese of Qu'Appelle, January 2019.

10   *The General Instruction of the Roman Missal* (Ottawa: Canadian Conference of Catholic Bishops, 2011), p. 35.

11   *Common Worship: Services and Prayers for the Church of England* (London: Church House Publishing, 2000), p. 158.

12   *The Deacon at Mass: A Theological and Pastoral Guide*, Second Edition (New York: Paulist Press, 2013), p. 1.

13   *The Liturgical Ministry of Deacons*, Second Edition (Collegeville: Liturgical Press, 2005), pp. 14–15.

14   *The Deacon's Ministry of the Liturgy* (Collegeville: Liturgical Press, 2016), p. 43.

15   W. Shawn McKnight, "The Uniqueness of the Deacon", in Keating (ed.), *The Character of the Deacon*, pp. 79–80.

16   *The Deacon's Ministry of the Liturgy*, p. 20.

17   *Many Servants*, First Edition, p. 61.

18   "Through the Dust".

19   *How Not to Say Mass*, Revised Edition (New York: Paulist Press, 2003), p. 42.

20   "The Diaconate as Ecumenical Opportunity".

21   *The Liturgical Ministry of Deacons*, pp. 71–77.

22   *The Deacon's Ministry of the Liturgy*, p. 73.

23   Ibid., p. 5.

Forming Deacons

CHAPTER 17

Challenges to Diaconal Formation in the Scottish Episcopal Church

Alison Peden

Introduction

I want to address in this chapter some of the challenges the Scottish Episcopal Church (SEC) faces in the formation of its deacons and how we are not only finding solutions, but also discovering blessings. The formation of our clergy is counter-cultural. As we nurture the vocations of deacons—and indeed priests—we are swimming against the tide of the world around them. The dominant narrative of our post-modern Western society is that of the task of creating our own identity: "I can be whatever and whoever I want to be."[1]

The Church has a different perspective: it calls people to become members of a community of faith, which will shape them according to its living traditions and values. Disciples seek to be formed in the Christian virtues of love, self-giving, generosity and sacrifice. All Christians are called to become more Christ-like in all that they do and say and believe. Likewise, our ordained ministers are called to model the example of Christ in their lives and help the Church in its vocation to become Christ-like.[2]

The most important element in formation is the creation of godly *habitus*, a disposition of Christ-likeness. A truly Christian character will shape the learning of ministers and enable them to be practitioners who reflect the values and virtues of the Church and in turn to inspire and develop those values in a way that grows authentically from the Christian tradition and Christ himself.[3] So it is in relation to this theme of formation of Christian character and disposition that I want to look at three areas of formation in the Scottish Episcopal Church and how deacon candidates have an impact on them.

Education

All our students train together in our Scottish Episcopal Institute—lay reader, deacon, and priest candidates. We usually have around thirty in the Institute community, and we currently have four training to be deacons. They come with a variety of previous experience and qualifications. Some are studying for higher degrees in theology; some have no further education at all. They all follow a suite of curricula designed by Durham University in England called "Common Awards".[4] These cover the expected elements of teaching curricula for ministry, such as Christian tradition, Bible, ethics, field education, and so on. We can tailor these Common Awards modules to our Scottish context, but they are not designed for any particular ministry—e.g. diaconal or priestly. So it can be a challenge to ensure that our diaconal candidates get the specific training that they need for their future ministry.

To some extent, we can look outside our classrooms for appropriate skills training. One of our diaconal candidates is already a graduate in divinity, so she is studying for a Master's degree in Practical Theology at Aberdeen University. Another will take a special course on ministry among older people at a Methodist lay training college, as that is her particular focus of ministry. Diaconal skills are also honed in placements, which are carefully chosen for each candidate—and we require diaconal candidates to do placements in congregations as well as sector ministry, so that the deacon can learn how to model Christ's *diakonia* in the liturgy and how to enthuse the people of God with a desire to grow the kingdom in their community.

Forming lay readers, priests and deacons together in a community reveals a delicate tension between this specialized skill-based learning and the character-formation that I described above. It has often been argued that it is difficult to describe the role of a deacon, because the role emerges with each individual in their God-given context. By contrast, the role of a priest or a lay reader is much more clear-cut and their context (the local congregation) is more pre-determined. So it is easier to determine which skills the priest or lay reader needs than the ones that a deacon needs. Yet it is in precisely this situation that we have found a gift that our deacon candidates offer to the learning community: our deacon candidates focus on developing a *character* that will provide them with a robust foundation for *whatever* ministry they undertake in whatever context. No one formational course can equip each deacon with what they need in terms of skills-knowledge. But it can offer them a community in which their disposition is nurtured.

Here, I want to draw on the insights of the Principal of our Institute, Canon Anne Tomlinson, who is herself a lifelong deacon.[5] The Principal described the character—the root disposition—of the deacon as embodying poverty of spirit, which includes:

- Seeing the capacities we have as gifts from God and being free enough to offer these to the service of God and others and to let go of them when they get in the way of that self-giving.
- Expressing the "John the Baptist principle": He must increase, but I must decrease. Deacons seek the enlargement of others through equipping and enabling them.
- Realizing that power *held* is dangerous—it will burn you up. Instead, we should see power as something which needs to flow safely through the making of connections *between* people—"a circuit". "Power with" rather than "power over".
- Seeing leadership as something that permeates the Body and is not individual. Trying to create leader*ful* organisations—where leadership capacity resides in every member, each of whom has to play her/his particular part.

As members of mixed classes and cell groups, the deacons are something of a leaven in the student lump. They remind the other students of the core, self-emptying character of Christ, his *diakonia*, which left him free of all self-concern to be bold, prophetic and strong. They remind us all that a Christ-like character is what enables *all* fruitful learning in ministry.

Community

A key aim of our formation programmes is to build community, as the crucible in which vocations are nurtured. Educational theory now is clear that the learning community, embodying particular values, is a vital factor in the effective training of practitioners. It shapes not only how we learn, but what we learn and absorb and assimilate. The Scottish Episcopal Institute is our community of formation. There are obvious practical difficulties for building a community that is geographically far-flung and diverse in its membership.

One of the challenges it poses is how to create a virtual learning community. Although our students come together for five training weekends, much of the teaching is delivered by Skype (soon to switch to "Big Blue Button"). The lecturer may be hundreds of miles away from the student, and the quality of broadband may not be as good as it should be. So, to develop our virtual learning community, we take care to train both teachers and students in "virtual etiquette"—how to ensure that you do not just speak to those in the room with you, but also those at a distance; how to wait for responses and make an effort to listen, share, debate and encourage. It is a good lesson in self-giving and collaboration—developing Christian disposition and *habitus*.

Another way of building a community from scattered elements is to pay particular attention to times when the community does assemble physically. Although there is plenty of learning and at least some socializing, we place a strong emphasis on praying together. The community gathers as a whole three times a day over the weekend for worship, and each student belongs to a cell/prayer group who also say Compline together. When a student—or member of staff—is in need of prayer, the community is alerted.

These are all ways in which community is built, and prospective deacons share in that community along with the others and are shaped by it. But again, we find one particular dimension of community formation in which the deacons have a particular gift to offer and make a particular impact. Our formation is designed to create reflective practitioners of Christian ministry and so theological reflection is a core element of the course. Theological reflection aims to integrate practical experience and academic disciplines so as to generate in the student a practical wisdom (*phronesis*) that they can deploy in ministry. *Phronesis* has been described as "the ability to intuit the relationship between the features of a particular situation and a general rule, and then to respond flexibly in the light of the rule but as the situation demands".[6] We develop it by paying substantial and serious attention to field education modules. Students are taught methods of theological reflection on their experience and are required to make presentations, engage with their peers in reflection and write up case studies and verbatims.

Quite a few of our students—especially candidates for priesthood—come along with theology degrees or are studying for them full-time. They inhabit the "hard, high ground" of theory and technique.[7] Such students can find it difficult to make their theology come alive in reflecting on their experience of, for example, a placement they are undertaking.[8] But those who discern a call to the diaconate are different. Deacon candidates are people who have *already* immersed themselves in what Donald Schön called "the swampy lowland", where "the problems of real-world practice do not present themselves to practitioners as well-formed structures . . . [or] as problems at all, but as messy, indeterminate situations".[9]

Moreover, deacon candidates have *already* had to think about their practice and experience in a theologically reflective way. When they enter the discernment process, often already engaged in some kind of missional outreach, they have to explain *why* the advocacy or caring or enabling that they are doing is a sign that they are called to *diaconal ministry*, rather than party-political campaigning or social work. That is, our deacon candidates have already had to *theologize* their experience in order to explain and substantiate their vocation to be deacons. They inhabit those "swampy lowlands", where most people live, identifying God's presence in them and reflecting on why what they are doing is *diakonia* in God's name.

Theological reflection is what deacons do incredibly well, and, as they grow as heralds of the kingdom, naming their work and their practice in gospel terms becomes habitual; they are living theological reflectors. Thus, they enable the community to grow through their sharing of this gift and model the kind of reflective practice that is sustained by community formation and develops through "companionship and collaboration".[10]

Vocation

The third challenge for us in forming deacons in the Scottish Episcopal Institute is vocational. It is easy for four deacons to be overshadowed by twenty or more priest and lay reader candidates. There are certain ways that we can solve this problem by affirming the distinct vocations. For example, we have a session on "vocational identity", which seeks to get the students thinking about who does what and where on a Sunday (if there were to be a deacon, a reader and a priest in a congregation) and then asks them to unpack what this tells us about the different ministries for which they are being formed.[11] This helps all our students to work out how to collaborate fruitfully in the future.

But finding models and exemplars for our diaconal candidates is difficult. We do not have enough able, local serving deacons to bring along to training weekends. We do not have enough deacons to provide good mentoring in curacies. We do not have enough deacons for our students to observe ordained diaconal ministry in practice. We are enormously grateful for offers of placements and mentoring from members of the Anglican Church of Canada and the Episcopal Church of the United States which will enlarge our candidates' perspectives. So the blessing that has emerged from the vocational challenge we face for our cohort of deacons is to make us turn outwards for help and thereby discover new friends. That is very much the charism of the Scottish Episcopal Church as a whole: we know our need of others and rejoice to encounter others and be nourished by them. Then we return to what is our own special context with renewed appreciation of what is distinct about it and an awareness of what we, in turn, can offer to others.

As we face the challenges of building community out of a scattered group of students, of finding ways to offer them the learning they need, and of clarifying and affirming their vocations, we have had to pay attention: attention to ways of relating to each other; attention to what a student really needs to learn; attention to how others can help in the quest to form ministers for building God's kingdom. And out of that attention have come blessings from our deacon candidates: a willingness to form character and disposition before anything else; a natural ability to find God in what they do; and an entrée into other communities that enrich our Province. We are praying earnestly for more deacon candidates, because they are needed for the formation of all the others.

Notes

[1] Anthony Giddens, *Modernity and Self-identity: Self and Society in the Late Modern Age* (Oxford: Polity Press, 1991), ch. 3, "The trajectory of the self", esp. pp. 74–80.

[2] David Heywood, "Educating ministers of character: building character into the learning process in ministerial formation", *Journal of Adult Theological Education* 10.1 (2013), pp. 4–24, here: p. 6.

[3] Cf. Barbara Fleischer, "Virtues and praxis in ministry education", *Reflective Practice: Formation and Supervision in Ministry* 32 (2012), pp. 171–183 (open access at <http://journals.sfu.ca/rpfs/index.php/rpfs>).

[4] See <https://www.dur.ac.uk/common.awards>.

[5] Canon Anne Tomlinson, "Where you stand is how you lead", *Germinate Lecture 2017*, available at <https://germinate.net/training/germinate-leadership/germinate-lecture/>.

[6] Heywood (above, n. 2), "Educating ministers of character", p. 8.

[7] Donald Schön, *Educating the Reflective Practitioner: Toward a New Design for Teaching and Learning in the Professions* (San Francisco: Jossey-Bass, 1987), p. 3.

[8] Jeremy Worthen, *Responding to God's Call: Christian Formation Today* (Norwich: Canterbury Press, 2012), pp. 136–139.

[9] Schön (above, n. 7), p. 4.

[10] Worthen (above, n. 8), pp. 140–141; cf. Nigel Rooms, "Paul as Practical Theologian: *Phronesis* in Philippians", *Practical Theology* 5:1 (2012), pp. 81–94; here: p. 84.

[11] See "Ministries in the Scottish Episcopal Church", a document reached through the first link on the SEC webpage at <https://www.scotland.anglican.org/who-we-are/vocation-and-ministry/ministry-scottish-episcopal-church>.

CHAPTER 18

Roman Catholic Diaconal Formation in Canada

George E. Newman

There are two streams which lead to ordination as a deacon in the Roman Catholic Church. The one which is most prominent in people's minds is the road that leads to priesthood, in which the man is first ordained as a deacon prior to being ordained as a priest. This is called the *transitional diaconate*. The second is the more recent programme for married men who intend to make diaconate a permanent position, the *permanent diaconate*. The selection process for each is different, and the areas of formation are also quite different.

Admissions/selection process

Transitional deacon
In the selection of men for this process, it is important to be sure there are no impediments for ordination, that the man is baptized and has received all the sacraments suitable for his age. It is also a good idea to make sure the man has the right attitude, in that he understands to what he is committing. In today's society, it will be important to be sure that he has a clear background, no lawsuits against him, any outstanding warrants or liabilities, no impropriety, and is not previously married. Checking his academic background is important also, since the studies will be long and difficult, and we need to be assured that the man has the ability to comprehend what will be taught. Obviously, besides other

references it will be important to consider the pastor's approval. If the pastor does not know the man, we have to wonder how much time the man spends participating in the sacraments.

Permanent deacon

Again, it is important to check that there are no impediments, that he has the right attitude, has a clear background, the ability to comprehend the studies, that he has his wife's approval, that he has his family's acceptance, has good references, his pastor's approval, and has deacon talent. I mention deacon talent, since it is one of the obvious, yet less well understood, aspects of the diaconate. The Selection Research Incorporated Company designed a questionnaire which helps to identify the talent for various positions. There is a "Deacon Perceiver" interview, a "Priest Perceiver" interview, and a "Teacher Perceiver" interview, as well as a "Religious Administrator" interview. Each of these is designed to identify the specific talents needed for each particular job. The Deacon Perceiver interview is being used by a dozen dioceses across Canada. Interestingly, the Priest Perceiver is not used by any diocese that I know of.

The emphasis on selecting the right people for the job has been a major factor in the selection process for permanent deacons from the beginning. This is a major difference between the selection of permanent deacons and transitional deacons. Because the transitional deacon is not going to engage in the traditional ministry of the deacon, the talents to be a deacon are not seen as important in the selection process. One would be led to wonder, if he is not going to engage in traditional deacon ministry, why ordain him as a deacon?

Basically, what is the difference between a *transitional deacon* and a *permanent deacon*? I think the major difference is what they are being called to do. The *permanent deacon* has a threefold ministry: the Word, Liturgy and Service. His formation is geared toward preparing him for this threefold ministry. Throughout the formation process there will be obvious differences.

In the case of *transitional deacons*, the objective of formation is ordination to priesthood, with leadership and parish management as well as liturgical expertise being paramount, with the result that the academic formation will receive the most attention. During the formation of the *permanent deacon*, the emphasis will be on personal development and human formation. This will be accomplished through enhancing diaconal talent, the ability to make changes, a growth in self-understanding, an increase in humility, recognition of personal abilities and limitations, improved relating ability and interpersonal skills. The assistance of the man's wife is of paramount importance. If the wife engages the formation process with her husband, the formation process will be more complete. The man will become a better deacon, if the wife engages the human formation aspects with him.

This will not come as a surprise to any married person. The married man who aspires to diaconate has already been in formation for many years. Marriage is probably the foremost formation process that he will ever undertake. If he understands that, and listens to his wife, he will know that this new formation will make him a better person and a better husband. He needs to engage the formation process the same way he engaged being married.

Discernment process

The discernment process will also have differences. In the case of the permanent deacon, extra emphasis is placed on the ability to accept rejection, improving his social interaction, speaking and communicating skills, and acceptance by classmates.

One of the important facets of discernment is having the men point out to one another what areas of their personality would be helpful as a deacon. On the flip side, they are asked to point out what aspects of their personality would be detrimental in ministry. This project is done without the attendance of the wives. Married couples do not want to hear what is wrong with their partner. They already know, but they do not want to hear it from someone else! For almost all of the men, this came as a wake-up call to the realization that there were things their wife had been telling them for years that needed to be fixed! Now that someone else could see it, it really made a big impact.

In my years at St Augustine's Seminary in Toronto, I worked closely with the men who were preparing for priesthood. Part of my job was helping them with budgets, writing essays and letters, and showing them how to take control of the calendar. One of the more enjoyable responsibilities I had was meeting the young men when they first arrived at the seminary and getting them settled. I would show them around, lead them through the annual calendar which we had prepared for them and arrange their first meeting with the rector.

On the second evening of their stay, I would explain the permanent diaconate to them. On the following weekend they would be meeting the men and their wives of the permanent diaconate who were also studying at the seminary. For most of these young men it was the first time they had met a permanent deacon and heard what our role in the Church was. I must say that they were very enthusiastic about our role and how we could work together in the parish.

Throughout the year they would often see me as the deacon at liturgies and begin to understand the role that they would take as deacon, reading the Gospel, and offering the intercessions. Occasionally I would also preach so they could see how the approach to scripture would differ between the perspectives of permanent and transitional deacons. I still remember the first time I preached to the seminary community. I began by saying, "I am going to say something from this pulpit which has never been said before in the whole history of this seminary." I could see everyone straighten up and pay attention, especially the faculty members. And then I began, "Just recently . . . *my wife and I* . . .". Sighs of relief and great chuckling. A married man had never preached from that pulpit before, and they all caught on right away.

Formation interaction

Meeting at meals with the married men and wives was a good experience for these young men. They had the opportunity to discuss academic topics as well as exchange ideas about raising families and the difficulties that married couples had with children as they grew and matured. I think the interfacing of these two groups was also a maturing aspect of their formation. The fact that there were also previously-ordained deacons acting as mentors with the candidates was an opportunity for both groups to learn what types of ministry were available, how it was handled, what difficulties arose and how to deal with difficult people.

Discernment of transitional deacons

One of my responsibilities was compiling the comments from faculty about each seminarian. Most of the comments were related to academic work and very little about their ability to socialize or display emotions. I found in this a strong contrast to the permanent diaconate discernment process. This may be because the focus of formation was different and the opportunity for socializing was not as readily available as it was for the permanent diaconate candidates.

Comparisons

The academic portion of the formation process was very similar for both types of deacons, with the addition of a six-month practicum for the permanent deacon candidate at a local hospital under the supervision of a qualified Clinical Pastoral Education Supervisor. Since the academic qualifications are not as strict for acceptance as a permanent deacon, life experience and additional courses taken in the workplace are taken into consideration. The formal length of time in formation for transitional deacons was four years of full-time study in theology after completion of an undergraduate degree.

The permanent deacon was in formation for four years on a part-time basis, consisting of one study weekend per month and one evening per week of group discussion and consideration of the questions on the academic topic of the month. The prospective permanent deacon was accepted into formation in a candidacy ceremony early in his first year of formation. Each group of candidates was under the guidance of a deacon mentor couple, who assisted them in the studies and gave an example of the type of interaction one would expect in dealing with parishioners.

The role of the mentor was one of the strong formation aspects of the programme and the selection of mentors who had cooperating wives was a major contributor to the success of the programme. The transitional deacons had their own formation groups which met regularly for discussion with their faculty supervisor.

Because the goal of each type of deacon was different, the methodology of the formation process was also different. The emphasis was on one being in leadership and teaching, as opposed to ministry and being present to those on the margins of society. While the priest has a fixed role in the parish, the deacon is flexible and will turn his hand to any ministry that needs help. Each deacon chooses the ministry to which he feels called and with the permission of his bishop he arranges this with the ministry supervisor, the volunteer coordinator, or whoever is responsible for visiting volunteer ministers. He is responsible for his own commitment of time; is considered a volunteer, so does not get paid; designs his own ministry format; and is responsible for attending an annual retreat with his wife. The retreat is paid for by his parish.

His activity in the parish is by agreement with the pastor and may include preaching, baptisms, weddings, funerals and vigils as well as being the deacon at Sunday eucharistic celebrations. He may also assist with programmes for the Rite of Christian Initiation of Adults (RCIA), interviewing couples for marriage and baptism, preside at Communion services, Stations of the Cross during Lent, benedictions, and exposition of the Blessed Sacrament, assist with prayer services, and any other needs that the pastor has.

As it was at the beginnings of the diaconate, Acts 6, the deacon is the bishop's man and offers to fulfil that responsibility to his pastor.

CHAPTER 19

Dimensions of Design for Deacon: Education and Formation

Josephine Borgeson

For more than forty years I have been involved in fostering the development of deacons and other ministry leaders; planning curricula, courses and workshops; teaching, consulting and mentoring, and advocating systemic change in the way we do ministry education. What I offer here are five questions to ask when beginning programme design.

What do we mean by formation?

Over the last few decades the phrase "faith formation" has replaced "religious education" in the Episcopal Church in the United States. I recognize that "formation" has a much longer history in Roman Catholicism, particularly when speaking of preparation for ordination and the religious life. But I admit to being a fan of "education" as a more comprehensive term. I sense that the emphasis on formation has become more important as we have recognized that Christendom is over and our communities are diverse and too often fragmented. Formation addresses our concerns with belonging and identity. Unfortunately, for many people education means only schooling.

Formation thus has become an effective term for describing the process of those called to be deacons as they explore questions of identity, attitudes, values and virtues central to their vocation. But there are two other dimensions of ministry education. One is the development of skills, that part of a programme or curriculum which can appropriately be spoken of as "training". The other is the acquisition of information and concepts. As we have shifted away from programmes heavy in traditional academic approaches, it is important to review our designs for learning for integration and a balance of training, working with ideas and formation, all the while respecting the gifts and experience which learners bring.

Where do we begin?

We begin by changing the direction of the flow of educational planning. Instead of goal, objective, learning activity, assessment, we begin with thinking about how we will assess learning.

In the work of the Committee on Vocational Formation and Lifelong Learning of the Association for Episcopal Deacons (AED), we have found that the biggest challenge is shifting the understanding of how we assess readiness for ordination. Even within one diocese, those planning and overseeing and teaching in the programmes for candidates may be disconnected from those in authority who assess learning. The caricature would be the progressive programme using individual learning plans, best adult education practices, heavy on mentored experiential learning, but working with a commission on ministry which administers a written canonical exam with multiple choice and essay questions. So as we begin to plan by talking about how assessment will be done, it is important for those who will do the teaching and mentoring to be in dialogue with those who will do the assessing. When we have a framework of competencies, as both the Anglican Church of Canada and the AED do, we have already set the tone for assessment. Assessment will be based on what the candidates can do, and that is what the competency documents describe. The competencies also provide a guide for deacons in forming their continuing learning goals after ordination.

How does planning unfold?

For individualized learning plans, or for the learning plan for a ministry team in a congregation, envision a grid with competencies described in a column down the left side of the grid. Then consider these headings running across the top of the grid, to be filled in for each of the competencies:

- *What I/we can do.* Often we ask about prior study, but the emphasis here is on what has been learned that is actually being used now in ministry.
- *What I/we need to learn.* What particular things will be focused on in this area of competence? Most of our competency documents are quite broad and expressed from the perspective of the dominant culture. Learning goals usually need to be more specific, articulated in a way that is sensitive to the context and culture of the learners.
- *How I/we will show what I/we learned.* This is a place to indicate what evidence of learning will be used in the process of assessment. Often learners are compiling portfolios which may be paper-based but more often are electronically assembled or a combination of electronic and print media. The latter allow more flexibility in the artifacts that may be included to show learning.
- *Learning activities to pursue my/our learning goals.* The last thing to focus on is specific learning activities and resources. When we begin an area for learning by shopping resources, we may have some interesting side-trips but we usually miss meeting the implied learning goal and confuse the assessment process. Resources and opportunities chosen after goals are clear are much more likely to result in lasting and useful learning, that is, competency.

What format or platform shall we use to enable learning?

Working through all those other columns before choosing learning resources will also give us a feel for what format or platform will be best to achieve learning goals and demonstrate learning. We have lots of choices today, thanks to electronic and telecommunication wonders, and the choices keep increasing. Any list of formats one could build would be obsolete immediately, but here are some of the ways I have taught, mentored, studied and facilitated in the last few years:

- working one to one, both face to face and using the telephone;
- in a massive open online course (mooc) as a learner, and with a few others in the same course, furthering conversation in an email group;
- using group blogs for dispersed book study groups;
- facilitating online asynchronous small group courses;
- leading live in classroom teaching;
- creating a classroom from a distance, using Skype, Zoom or Google Hangouts, supported by Google Classroom.

Who is a part of the learning community?

It is important to consider who makes up the learning community for those preparing to be deacons, and for deacons in their pursuit of lifelong learning and development, because the need for deacons to have a sense of diaconal community, or mutual support among those who share a vocation, must be weighed against the need for ministry teams and ministering communities which work and learn together.

In the Episcopal Church there are several strands which have done one or the other of these very well. We have inherited a great tradition from the deaconess training programmes, whose graduates, as they went about their ministries, often functioned more like dispersed religious communities. They enjoyed a strong sense of support, remembering one another in prayer regularly, staying in touch by letters and reuniting periodically. There are deacon programmes today which work very hard at building community feeling among cohorts of graduates.

Where I began my work in ministry education, in the Episcopal Diocese of Nevada, we located our teaching and learning communities in the congregation or a cluster of nearby congregations which shared a context for ministry. Everyone, regardless of specific call, studied together. There was little separate study done around the ordained offices, but differentiation in identity and roles happened anyway. Experiencing deacon and presbyter ministry developers working together, educationally and liturgically, helped. Other dioceses which have known only presbyters in local ministry development and education roles have needed to add extra teaching and mentoring for those called to be deacon.

Drawing on what we can learn from the varieties of diocesan programmes and reviewing what we mean by formation, we can suggest what the appropriate learning community might be. When we think about *formation* in ministry, we see that there is a need to deepen understanding of the general baptismal call to ministry for everyone, but also to enrich and develop the specific identify and attitudes in those called to be deacons. When we think about developing *skills* for ministry, we see that the best efforts teach some foundational skills to everyone and provide opportunities for further skill development based on the gifts and callings of individuals.

And when it comes to *concepts and information*, to scripture, history and theology, we have learned it is best to have those who will be ministering together learn and reflect together, developing a common base of understanding faith traditions. In this way they build relationships, equipping them for continuing ministry and conversation.

Notes

Competencies from AED may be found here: <https://www.episcopal deacons.org/deacon-competencies.html>. Find other resources related to formation and lifelong learning for deacons on the same website.

The *Iona Report* from the Anglican Church of Canada with competencies for deacons may be found here: <https://www.anglican.ca/wp-content/uploads/iona-report.pdf>.